PENGUIN BOOKS

Gulp!

'An honest, authentic and inspiring guide to listening to your heart, facing your fears and following your dreams. This book is excellent for anyone at a crossroads in their life.' *Nick Williams, founder of Heart at Work London, co-founder of Dreambuilders Community, a trustee director of Alternatives, and author of* The Work We Were Born To Do, Unconditional Success, Powerful Beyond Measure *and* How To Be Inspired

'Gulp! – read this book and there really are no more excuses for not living and having the life you really want. This brilliant programme gives us a practical roadmap of how to transform fear into inspired action – in just seven days.' *Suzy Greaves, bestselling author of* Making the Big Leap

'Gabriella is fantastic at helping you think outside the box.' *Nicky Hambleton-Jones, Presenter of Channel 4's* 10 Years Younger

'Hold on to your hat, this will be the ride of your life.' *Sarah Newton, presenter of ITV2's* My Teen's a Nightmare – I'm Moving Out!

'Reading *Gulp!* is like having a best friend with wonderful inspiration, clarity and compassion. Gabriella is an expert at helping you find out where you *really* want to go in life and how you get there.' *Bob Griffiths, author of* Grow Your Own Carrot

'Gabriella exudes such positive energy, creativity and compassion. Highly intuitive, she balances a natural sense of fun with the serious business of helping people achieve genuine results.' *Carole Gaskell, bestselling author of* Transform Your Life *and* Pocket Life Coach

Gulp!

The seven-day crash course to master fear and break through any challenge

GABRIELLA GODDARD

PENGUIN BOOKS

PENGUIN BOOKS

Published by the Penguin Group
Penguin Books Ltd, 80 Strand, London WC2R 0RL, England
Penguin Group (USA) Inc., 375 Hudson Street, New York, New York 10014, USA
Penguin Group (Canada), 90 Eglinton Avenue East, Suite 700, Toronto, Ontario, Canada M4P 2Y3
(a division of Pearson Penguin Canada Inc.)
Penguin Ireland, 25 St Stephen's Green, Dublin 2, Ireland (a division of Penguin Books Ltd)
Penguin Group (Australia), 250 Camberwell Road, Camberwell,
Victoria 3124, Australia (a division of Pearson Australia Group Pty Ltd)
Penguin Books India Pvt Ltd, 11 Community Centre, Panchsheel Park, New Delhi – 110 017, India
Penguin Group (NZ), cnr Airborne and Rosedale Roads, Albany,
Auckland 1310, New Zealand (a division of Pearson New Zealand Ltd)
Penguin Books (South Africa) (Pty) Ltd, 24 Sturdee Avenue,
Rosebank, Johannesburg 2196, South Africa

Penguin Books Ltd, Registered Offices: 80 Strand, London WC2R 0RL, England

www.penguin.com

First published 2006
1

Set in 12.5/14.75 pt Monotype Fournier
Typeset by Rowland Phototypesetting Ltd, Bury St Edmunds, Suffolk
Printed in England by Clays Ltd, St Ives plc

ISBN-13: 978–0–141–02528–5
ISBN-10: 0–141–02528–X

The veil of confusion gently falls away,
Like the dank mist on a dull winter's day.
Revealing the path that lies there before me,
To step forward or not, what will it be?

If not now . . . when?

Contents

Acknowledgements

When I was seven years old, I dreamed of writing a book. Somehow that dream got lost in what we call 'life'. It wasn't until The Lump turned up and the ensuing threat of cancer that I dusted off the cover of this particular dream and decided to do something about it.

Thank you to Julia McCutchen for your wonderful guidance and mentoring which gave me the confidence to get started on my writer's journey.[1] I am truly grateful for all your support and encouragement.

Thank you to my agent Jacqueline Burns, for all your patience and incredible intuitive and creative sparks. Thank you to Kate Adams and the team at Penguin, for biting the bullet and taking the punt on me, and for your pivotal role in getting Gulp! out into the world. And thank you also to Fiona Brown for your masterful editing and for smoothing off the rough edges.

Thank you to Stuart Laycock for bringing Gulp! to life in visual design and for your fabulous illustrations, and to Kate Bacon, my personal assistant, for all your support and your eternally bright disposition.

Thank you to all my friends, family and colleagues for all those philosophical discussions about life, love and everything else under the sun. Special thanks to Surekha Aggarwal, Ushma Patel, Gail Bradley, Nick Williams, Carole Gaskell, Sue Ingram, Veronica Lim, Anita Patel, Margaret-Jane Howe, Rhian Pamphilon, Elaine and Clive Broadbent, Janet Limb, Gerda Druks-Kok, Altazar Rossiter, Rick Trask, Linda Taylor, Jo Goddard, Angela Goddard, Margaretanne Roger, Pauline Templeman, Sue Goddard, John Adam, Hannah Pursall, Carmen Carreno, Lucia Gaitan, Sharon Henaghan and Jeremy Lazarus.

Thank you to all the brave souls who shared their stories for this book, and to all my clients over the past years. You know who you are. You are wonderful and amazing beings. Our work together has always inspired and challenged me to question everything and constantly grow and evolve so that I can be making the best contribution I can while I'm alive and kicking on this earth.

Thank you to Jean Warren for being the best neighbour in the world and for all the surprise deliveries of jelly and ice-cream, chocolate bars and tuna salads to keep my belly full and my spirits high while writing this book.

Thank you also to my furry four-legged friends Bo and Tatiana. Thank you so much for your unconditional love and affection over our years together. Les quiero muchisimo.

Finally, special thanks to Yvonne, my Mum, for being an inspirational role model and showing such courage in the face of challenge as you follow your true calling, and to Chris, my Dad, for your curious and inquisitive mind and inventive spirit. The fruits of your labours live and breathe in every page of this book.

Introduction

Gulp! Aims

To inspire you to
face your fear,
step up to the challenge,
and move through your Gulp! calmly,
swiftly and gracefully.

Gulp! Time

Sometimes in life, a challenge crops up that calls for you to step outside your comfort zone. You feel the fear in the pit of your stomach. You know in your heart of hearts that it's time to bite the bullet and face the challenge. But you're afraid. You're worried things will go wrong, and that you might fall flat on your face. Yet at the same time there is a faint glimmer of excitement and anticipation bubbling beneath the fear. Deep down, you know it is time to *do* something, to make a change. It's crunch time. It's time to step up to the challenge and break through the fear that holds you back. And it's time to leap to the next level of your life.

When you feel challenged, it's because there is something in the situation that is causing you to question who you are and how you believe the world should be. Now, you always have a choice. You can meet your challenge head on and step up to it. Or you can shy away from it and hope it will go away. But the truth is, it won't ever go away. If you don't deal with it now, it will come back and find you again in a different time, a different place and a different situation. So you have a choice. Deal with it now? Or deal with it later?

The choice is yours.

When you choose to face your Gulp! you are taking an important step forward in your own personal growth and development. It is a process of transformation and I'm delighted to be here partnering with you on your journey. It will really open your eyes and heighten your awareness about who you are and what you're truly capable of. And it will force you to let go of the things that hold you back.

It is time to move to the next level of your potential.

Why Gulp!

Challenges happen for a reason. They come into our lives to teach us something, or to help us move through a block that is holding us back. They stretch us and call us to grow as human beings. They teach us how to trust ourselves. They take us out of the box that we've created for ourselves and force us to question the fundamental beliefs that we've used to shape who we think we are and what we believe we can achieve in this world. And they provide us with the impetus to step out of the known and into the unknown where we can create anew.

According to The Oxford English Dictionary, the verb 'gulp' means *to swallow with difficulty in response to strong emotion.* Over the years I've worked with hundreds of people, helping them to find the inner courage and strength to make big changes in their lives. And what I've found is that there is always a defining moment; a distinct point in time where they decide that 'yes' they're going to meet the challenge and go through with it. More often than not, this is followed by a physical 'Gulp!'. And when I hear that sound, I smile. That's because I know that we're finally on track. I know that they've decided to face their fears and defy their demons. That they're ready to say 'yes' to living a rich and full life. And that they're ready to say 'No' to the situation they're in because they no longer want to settle for suffering or mediocrity, or for simply being a shadow of the person they know lives and breathes deep inside of them. The journey that ensues isn't always easy, but where they end up is a much better place, bringing with it a new sense of happiness, fulfilment and possibility.

Gulp! is for people who are ready to embrace their challenging situation head on. Maybe you've had a challenge thrust upon you, completely out of the blue and out of your control, and you have no choice but to embrace it. Or maybe you're simply tired of being stuck in a rut and feel like it's time to do something a bit different and radical. Whatever your situation, and no matter how big or small your challenge is, believe that you *can* get through it.

The Brewing Gulp!

You've been building up to it for a while now. What started out as a small itch of dissatisfaction has turned into a full-blown rash. You know that the time has come to do something about your situation. It won't go away and, unfortunately, nobody else will make the decision for you. Like Dave, who had a successful career in management consultancy working for a big name firm, but yearned to become a film director. Or Penny, who had been with her boyfriend for four years and wanted commitment and kids, or else she wanted out. Or like Maria, who had become increasingly resentful at work because her team's achievements weren't being recognized, and she knew it was time for her to raise her head above the parapet.

The Bombshell Gulp!

On the other hand, sometimes we're in the flow of life and something comes completely out of the blue that hits us on the head and brings us to a halt. We're not prepared for it, but we've got to deal with it. Often it calls for us to dig deep and find an inner courage and strength that we didn't even know we possessed. Like Clare when she discovered that her boyfriend, who had been discussing marriage, had slept with her best friend while she was working away. Or like Jean, who was leaning over in the bath washing her hair when she found a lump in her left breast. Or like Peter, whose boss called him at 8 in the morning and asked him to present the quarterly results at the senior management meeting because he'd put his back out at squash.

The Breakthrough Gulp!

And then there are the times when we simply get stuck in a rut. Life is good, but it's boring. We want a fresh challenge. We want to stretch ourselves. And we want to reenergize our life. Like Max, who took up salsa dancing and found a new lease of life and his soul mate in the process. Or Dan, who decided to forsake his usual boozy beach holiday for a challenging trek through the high altitudes of Tibet. Or Moira, who reconnected with her childhood talent for drawing, and started to design greetings cards in her spare time.

This is your life, so live it well. Why settle for anything less? Whatever your challenge, know that it's a call – a call to reconnect to what's truly important to you, a call to make the changes that you know deep down you need to make and a call to let go of anything or anyone that holds you back or no longer serves the best in you.

While I'm guessing that you've bought this book to address a specific challenge, my vision is that you adopt the Gulp! principles and practices and make them an integral part of everyday living. I would love it if you got into the habit of making 'a Gulp! a day'. It will help you grow as a person. It will empower you. It will create momentum in your life. And, most importantly, it will constantly open your mind to new and wonderful possibilities.

Gulp! Wisdom

A Gulp! a day keeps mediocrity at bay.

Gulp! Time

When to Gulp!

Change can be looming for a while before you even notice it. That's because it manifests itself in different ways. You might feel frustrated or stuck. Or you might be getting increasingly angry with the people around you. Or you might feel confused and a little lost, like you're caught between two worlds without a sure footing in either. The problem is that we're so busy living our lives and trying to get everything done that we often don't see the signs, or we notice them and ignore them because we're 'too busy right now'.

From my work with clients, here are twenty of the most common tell-tale symptoms which signal that change is needed:

1. Your energy levels are low and you lack oomph.
2. Deep down you feel you're selling yourself short.
3. You know you could be doing better.
4. You're tired and frustrated with holding yourself back.
5. You feel boxed in.
6. You feel jealous of successful people around you.
7. You find it hard to get up in the morning.
8. The people around you start to annoy you.
9. Your clothes don't feel right any more.
10. You feel listless and indecisive.

11. You feel stuck in a rut.
12. You feel short tempered and impatient.
13. You feel confused with no clear way forward.
14. You're tired and not sleeping well.
15. You easily lose concentration.
16. It seems like things are falling apart around you.
17. You haven't felt really happy for a while.
18. You *know* there's got to be a better way.
19. You're starting to consider new possibilities.
20. The grass starts to look greener on the other side.

Sometimes people put up with these symptoms because they fear the unknown and what might lie on the other side. But put up with any of these symptoms for an extended period of time without addressing them, and you'll find them manifesting themselves in different ways: you get sick, your performance at work goes down, you start drinking more, you overeat, your quick temper gets you into trouble. This 'dis-ease' in your life is your mind, body and soul's way of telling you that you are not being true to yourself.

What you resist persists, so don't ignore the signs any longer. Take this chance to embrace a life that challenges and stretches you, taking you to places that you never dreamed of before. Step outside the box that you've put yourself in, and step into the unknown where the only boundaries are the ones which you define. Break through the barriers you've erected around you. Leave behind what doesn't work any more and welcome brand new opportunities and possibilities into your life. Open yourself to chance, and allow chance to happen to you.

The choice is yours, and only yours.

Gulp! Wisdom

Change your life by changing yourself.

Gulp! Time

My Gulp!

They say that when the student is ready, the teacher comes, and I guess that Miguel was the right man at the right time. He was a Buddhist teacher in Mexico City who was trying to teach me the elusive art of meditation in the hope that it would calm my stressed out mind and body. One day he pointed his finger at my chest and said, 'It's time for you to live *your* life.' His innate wisdom was met with a blank stare because at the time I thought I *was* living my own life. I just nodded solemnly and went away thinking maybe I'd misunderstood his Spanish. Now when I look back at that moment over eleven years ago, I realize how right Miguel was.

I wasn't living my true life. As a high-flying international marketing executive I was burning myself out trying to meet deadlines and get results that didn't really matter to me. Years later when the broadband company I worked for went under, I was catapulted into the world of self-employment. That was my choice, I must add. I could have easily taken another marketing directorship, but something deep inside me urged me to go out on my own. True madness, really, because I'd just used up my hard-earned savings on buying a house in London.

Over the years that followed I retrained in coaching

skills and leadership, and read hundreds of books on self-development and personal development that must have kept Amazon in business. I've spent a lot of time exploring spirituality and what it means to me. My motto became 'Freedom lies in being bold' thanks to the late great Robert Frost. And boy, was I bold. I carved out a niche for myself as a specialist in personal branding, blending together my corporate branding experience with my new-found leadership and coaching skills. And I developed a strong client base of executives, corporate professionals, individuals, entrepreneurs, authors and even the odd celebrity. I was happy; each day was a new adventure and my life was well and truly on track. And then one day something happened that threw me completely off course, or rather 'on course' as it later turned out.

It was a crisp Tuesday morning in October when I found The Lump. At first I thought I was imagining it, but then as I ran my fingers over the skin above my thudding heart, I felt it again. It was like a hard oval baked bean lying just below the surface of my skin. And it was definitely there. I immediately felt numb, just like that feeling when you know it's your turn to speak in front of a large group. My stomach sank and then somersaulted back up into my throat. Surely I was too young to get breast cancer? I checked for The Lump again, just to make sure. It was definitely there.

Only twenty-four hours previously I had been blissfully ignorant of my predicament. Sitting at the table sipping my morning coffee I had been watching breakfast television, as I always do in the morning. It was breast cancer awareness month and the presenters were interviewing a young woman who had found a lump in her breast. By the time the woman finally did something about it, it was too late. She had had a mastectomy and was going through the process of breast reconstruction.

I felt very sorry for her, but was amazed at how upbeat she was. At one point, she turned her head to directly face the camera and said, 'Check now before it's too late.' It was weird. I felt she was looking directly at me. Of course I *knew* she couldn't see me, but I felt as if she was speaking straight to me. I remember thinking how odd it was, and went to wash up the dishes and feed the cats.

I thought nothing more of it until the next morning. I was watching a completely different breakfast TV show when the same young woman came on for an interview. When she looked into the camera, her hazel brown eyes meeting mine, I immediately felt guilty for not heeding her message the day before. I raced upstairs to my bedroom to do the breast check.

That's when I found The Lump. I didn't believe it at first. I tried again. It was definitely there.

Surely this couldn't happen to me?

I went back downstairs and the young woman was still sitting on the couch talking about her forthcoming breast reconstruction operation. Then she turned her head to look directly back into the camera. It was strange, as if she knew I was back again. 'If you find a lump, get it checked by your doctor,' she said. 'You never think it can happen to you – but it can. Do it now before it's too late.'

This time I did heed her warning and immediately made an appointment with my doctor. She confirmed my findings and referred me to a consultant at Guys Hospital. He immediately found The Lump, three centimetres long. How is it possible that these things are growing in our body and we don't even know about them? An appointment for a mammogram and ultrasound was booked – and so began the longest wait of my life.

Over the weeks that followed, my life was in turmoil. Since finding The Lump, I suddenly became aware of the implications it could have on my life. At first, I didn't think the worst. My biggest concern was that if The Lump was cancerous, I might have to have my breast removed. As I was actively looking for my life partner at the time, I was horrified at the thought of only having one boob! I mean, what would one say to a prospective partner? As time went on, my thoughts moved on to the greater implications it could have, and finally settled on the thought of death.

Now we all know we are going to die some time. But when the possibility is literally staring you in the face, it really puts life into perspective. I remember spending one weekend in the depths of depression, pleading with the greater forces above, telling them that I didn't want to die and that it wasn't time for me to go yet. I remember going to sit and watch the swans at the local dock, just enjoying the warmth of the sun and the beauty of a white swan as it went about its daily business of being alive. Could all this be taken away from me? What had I done wrong? Surely I was too young to get cancer?

It sounds a bit melodramatic now looking back, but those of you who have been in a similar situation will probably find this familiar.

That's when I really started to look at my own life. Was I living my true life? Was I being who I was born to be? Was I really doing the things that made my heart sing and my soul dance? What about my legacy? What was I going to leave behind when I died?

It was about that time that I decided that I wanted to be a writer.

Ever since I was a little girl, I had loved writing. Apparently, I had an incredible imagination as a child and my short stories won competitions. I even wrote the school play at the tender age of seven. Writing, for me, was a way of escaping into my own little world. But as I got older, it seems that common sense took over and I pursued a path of science and technology – because 'I'd never be out of a job'.

Sitting there watching the white swans glide effortlessly across the water, I asked myself, 'If not now . . . when?'

It's a great question, isn't it? It really gets you thinking. How often do we say, 'I'll do that when . . .'

- *I get older.*
- *I have more money.*
- *I find my life partner.*
- *I have more time.*
- *I feel more confident.*
- *I'm better at . . .*
- *Someone recognizes my talent.*

What happens if there is no WHEN? And more importantly, what's stopping you from being that person you want to be, or doing that thing you want to do . . . starting right here . . . right NOW?

I've realized that there is no time like the present, because there is nothing BUT the present. The past is over and the future is what we create it to be.

The only thing stopping you . . . is YOU. And I hope you never have to get a wake-up call like mine.

Thankfully, the hospital tests showed that The Lump was

in fact a cyst. I was going to keep my breast. And I was going to live. Such simple words to say, but so full of meaning when you realize that the choice of life or death is very rarely yours.

And so I began to write.

Now, hand on heart, I can say that my life is well and truly on track. Each day continues to be a new adventure, and each day brings with it situations that require me to step up and face a challenge. From screen testing for a TV show to speaking to a group of sixty journalists. From going on a blind date to pitching a seminar proposal to a senior executive of one of the top investment banks in the world. From sitting down and starting to write this book that you're reading to overcoming my embarrassment as I take my first singing lesson.

When I face a new challenge, I learn so much about myself. I stretch the boundaries and discover what I'm truly capable of and find strengths and talents I didn't even know I had. Sometimes I fall short of the mark. Other times I pass with flying colours and that gives me the confidence to meet the next challenge head on. But every time requires me to step through that elusive point – the Gulp! – when my heart is pounding and my stomach is fluttering, but deep down I *know* it is the right thing to do.

I often wished that there was a book that could support me and encourage me every time I had to face a challenging situation. While there are books written for specific situations like going on a job interview, giving a presentation, screen testing, writing a book and going on a date, I couldn't find one book that would help me find the courage and confidence to be ready for any type of challenge.

That's why I've written Gulp!. I want to inspire you to

embrace the challenges that crop up in your life. I want to help you to build a strong inner core and the confidence you need to face them head on. And I want you to feel supported and encouraged as you step up to them, knowing that there are hundreds of other readers doing exactly the same.

Because when you stretch yourself out of your comfort zone, you create space for miracles to happen.

Gulp! Wisdom

This is your life. Live it well.

Gulp! Time

How to Gulp!

The Gulp! philosophy is simple. Challenges are good. They're an opportunity to learn and grow. They give us a reason to stop and reflect upon what's really important to us. They open us to new ideas and opportunities. And they provide us with the impetus to make quantum shifts in our life.

One of my personal quirks is that I've long been fascinated by martial arts movies. One great influence was the 1970s television series called *Kung Fu*[1] starring David Carradine as Kwai Chang Caine, a young, orphaned Shaolin monk and an expert in the ancient Chinese art of Kung Fu. His guide and mentor, an old blind Shaolin priest named Master Po, referred to him as 'Grasshopper' and taught him about the nature of being and universal harmony. Caine himself was a softly spoken and gentle character, except of course when he needed to defend himself from a vicious bounty hunter or Chinese assassin. Waiting patiently with all senses alert, he would turn calmly and swiftly, taking on approaching assailants with little fanfare, and dealing with them artfully and gracefully. More modern-day movies like *Crouching Tiger, Hidden Dragon*[2] also display some exquisite examples of graceful and flowing Chinese martial arts scenes that blend stillness and alertness with the ability to act swiftly and elegantly.

Gulp! Wisdom

An attitude of alertness and inner calm is a most powerful weapon.

Takuan Soho, sixteenth-century Samurai

Gulp! Time

When faced with challenges in life, wouldn't it be great to be able to deal with them in the same way? Swiftly and elegantly! Wouldn't it be great to be so centred in yourself that the action you take is swift and right on target? Wouldn't it be reassuring to know that when you step outside your comfort zone and into the void of the unknown, you'll be able to deal with whatever comes up quickly and gracefully, because you are poised and balanced? And wouldn't it be fabulous to build a sense of inner calm so strong that it gives you the inner power to face even bigger gulps in your life?

That's why at the heart of the Gulp! philosophy is the importance of being able to calm the mind and build a strong inner core. True inner power comes from your mind and body being aligned and in sync with your soul. In the face of any challenge, this combination is formidable.

To help you face your challenge, I've created a seven-day programme with one simple aim – that when you step up to your challenge, you can approach it calmly, courageously and confidently, that you can move through it swiftly and gracefully, and that you land on the other side poised and balanced with both feet on the ground.

Day 1: Dare & Defy

The challenge is there, whether you like it or not. So what are you going to do about it? If you're not going to step up to it now, when will you? Day 1 is all about facing your challenge head on, exploring the deeper meaning beneath it, understanding the root of any pain or suffering and making the ultimate choice of 'go, or no go'.

Day 2: Breakdown & Breakthrough

The biggest thing holding you back is fear; fear of the unknown, fear of failure, and the list of fears goes on. The aim of Day 2 is to master this fear. We'll break it down and put it under the microscope so you can see it for what it really is. Then we'll explore ways that you can transform fear from a brake that slows you down into a propeller that moves you forward.

Day 3: Centre & Connect

Being connected to your centre and inner core is the fundamental foundation of the Gulp! philosophy. Only when you can silence your thoughts, can you connect to your deeper wisdom. Here there is no fear. Here there is

only what is aligned to your true essence and wha
right. In Day 3 you'll learn different ways to calm yo
mind and build a strong inner core. This will help you make better choices and decisions, and remain centred and strong when the pressure hits.

Day 4: Imagine & Invent

When you shut up the chit chat and fears that plague your mind, you create 'space' for new ideas and insights to emerge. What if this challenge is actually a catalyst? A once-in-a-lifetime chance for you to make a quantum shift in your life? The aim of Day 4 is to expand your mind and get you thinking outside the box. We'll get you brainstorming new ideas and looking at your challenge from completely new perspectives.

Day 5: Plan & Prepare

After stirring up this creativity, it's now time to chart your course and start to move forward. Day 5 is about defining where you're heading and what you need to do to get there. We'll look at what you know, what you don't know and what you need to find out. Then we'll identify clear and targeted actions which you can take to get you there swiftly and gracefully. And finally we'll explore ways that you can prepare yourself physically to keep your energy high as you head towards your Gulp!.

Day 6: Focus & Flow

As you step forward you move into the uncertainty of the unknown. Day 5 is all about encouraging you to let go of control and learn how to simply 'be in the flow' as you walk down that path. Today, we'll explore how intention, intuition and instinct can be powerful signposts to guide you. We'll also look at what you need to let go of in order to stay light and agile. And you'll learn how to alchemize any fear that might flare up in the moment.

Day 7: Gulp! & Go

By now, you'll realize that there's no turning back. You're moving forward. You're on the right path. And in many ways it might feel that the path is actually leading you. It's Gulp! time. The aim of Day 7 is to inspire you to make that final leap. We'll tie up any loose ends and then hear the stories of three people who, like you, have bitten the bullet, stepped up to the challenge and transformed their lives in the process.

Epilogue

So . . . if you can make this Gulp! . . . what else is possible?

Gulp! Wisdom

If my mind can conceive it, and my heart can believe it,
I know I can achieve it.
Reverend Jesse Jackson

Gulp! Time

How to Use this Book

The Gulp! you are facing is calling you to step out of your comfort zone and into unfamiliar territory. For some, it will be a big job interview, an audition, a first day at work or an important presentation or meeting. For others, it will be the day you get engaged, or married or even divorced. And for others, it'll be the day you break out and do something different, like dating again, embarking on an exciting adventure or quitting your job to retire or launch your own business.

Whatever the reason, it's important. It's crunch time. And it's looming. You want to be in top form. At the same time, there's that gnawing sense of self-doubt and fear deep within your belly. Will you be able to carry it off? Will it work out OK? What happens if you mess things up?

If you're starting to feel the panic building, just take a deep breath and keep reading. The strategies covered in this book are powerful, and will work wonders on improving your confidence and ability to cope with any challenge that life sends your way.

Working through Gulp! is easy. There are seven chapters, one for each day. Each one provides you with food for thought, inspiring stories, insightful questions and practical activities to help you successfully step through your challenge. For small challenges, ones that require you to dip a toe outside your comfort zone, you can follow the programme in a week. For bigger challenges that require upheaval and major shifts in your life, you may like to follow the programme over a period of a month or so, with one or two chapters a week.

At the end of each chapter there is a space for creating your own Gulp! Action Plan. The amount of preparation that you do will depend on the size of your Gulp! and how nervous the situation makes you feel. So at the end of each chapter, I've created some action suggestions for each of these three categories:

Gulp! Espresso

This is a short sharp Gulp! often made on the spur of the moment. Yet its impact is powerful. This is one of those everyday moments where you choose to do something differently, something that stretches you outside your comfort zone. Yes, it is nerve-racking, but no, it's not a life or death situation. It happens in the moment and requires little planning or preparation, just a bit of courage and conviction. Examples include: saying no when you'd normally say yes, asking someone out on a date, or signing up to a photography class on your own.

Gulp! Mediano

This can be a situation that has been bubbling for a while now. Deep down you know you need to address it and it will really mean stepping outside your comfort zone. While it won't result in a big change in your lifestyle, it will mean a shift in mentality leaving you stronger and more empowered. While part of you feels nervous at the thought of the situation, there is also a tingle of anticipation and excitement. Some planning, preparation and practice are required. Examples include: asking for a pay rise, speaking in public, getting engaged or standing up to a bully.

Gulp! Grande

This is when you take a quantum leap in your life, making a complete transformation. These are often highly stressful situations that need you to make big life-changing decisions. Sometimes you initiate them, other times they're thrust upon you. The change is often abrupt and can impact on your financial and personal well-being.

Sometimes they might even mean the difference between life and death. It requires a lot of planning and preparation and may take three to six months to pass through the change. Examples include: ditching your day job to start your own business, finding out you have cancer, deciding to leave your long-term partner or moving to a new country to make a fresh start.

Whatever your challenge, work at your own pace and go with the flow, because that's a key message of this book. All I recommend is that the first time you read this book, follow the chapters in sequence because each chapter has a different purpose, focus and energy. You are going on a journey, and each chapter prepares you mentally, emotionally and spiritually for the next step of your Gulp! When you've read it through once, you can then go back and dip in and out of the chapters.

As you embark on your Gulp! journey, remember to:

- Buy a special journal or notebook to write down your thoughts, and to record the insights and observations that crop up on your way.
- Take time out to complete the practical activities and reflection questions. You'll gain a greater understanding of yourself, your patterns and how you hold yourself back.
- Celebrate your wins. When you have a breakthrough or achieve a goal, no matter how big or small it is, make sure you acknowledge your success.

And yes, you can simply read this book and do nothing else. But if you really want to live a life where you're feeling fully alive, then make the commitment to putting these ideas into action and taking daily action.

Gulp! Wisdom

Just one step could change your life forever.

Gulp! Time

Extra Gulp! Support

Facing challenges can be daunting, so why not create a support team around you of like-minded people who can encourage you on your journey. They'll be honoured you asked. Be accountable to them, and ask them to hold you to your promises. In fact, why not find a small group of friends and work through the book together?

For extra support, and to help you connect with other readers from around the world who are also making their Gulp!, why not come and join us in the Gulp! Member's Area at www.gulptime.com.

Here you'll find:

- free tip sheets and action plan forms
- guidelines for setting up your own Gulp! Group
- the 'pledge page', where you commit to the whole wide world about your Gulp!
- on-line discussion forums
- inspirational stories from people who have made their Gulp!
- free telephone forums with the Gulp! Coaches

- options for regular email alerts and mobile alerts
- and much, much more . . .

How to Access the Gulp! Member's Area

1. Go to our website: http://www.gulptime.com
2. Click on the section that says 'Member's Zone'
3. Enter your name and email address in the spaces provided.
4. An email will be sent to you with your password and access details.

Gulp! Time

Final Words

I'd like to wish you the very best of luck as you step up to your Gulp! and embark on this journey of personal growth and development. As you begin, I'd like to leave you with these powerful words of encouragement that come from the Maori language,[3] the indigenous language of New Zealand.

Kia Kaha. Kia Toa.

Be Strong. Be Brave.

Gulp! Time

Remember that you are the creator of your life. And you create your future. So go create.

Gabriella Goddard, 2006

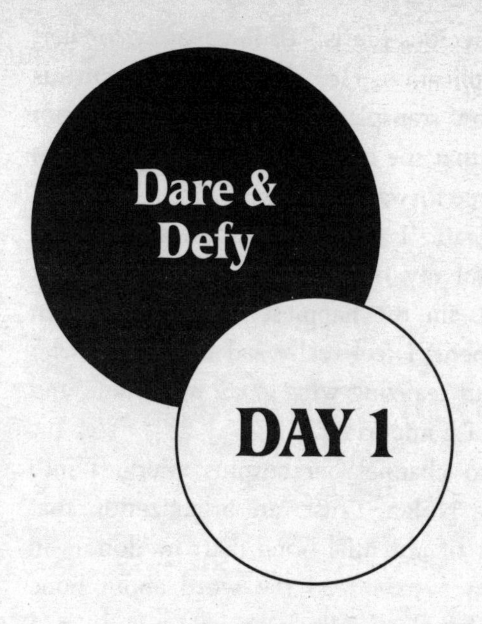

Gulp! Aims for Today

Name the challenge.
Understand the deeper meaning beneath it.
Make the choice to 'go', or 'no go'.

Gulp! Time

Sian was only twenty-nine when she was diagnosed with leukaemia. The shock was indescribable. Yet Sian believes that it has changed her life – for the better. 'This sounds strange I know, as I am only twenty-nine, and the condition that I have most commonly affects "old" men nearing the end of their lives,' she says. 'But in spite of all this, I feel incredibly lucky that I have been given a jolt which has made me realize just how precious life is.' Unfortunately for her, there's a further complication. Her only hope of a cure is to have a bone marrow transplant, and her brother is not a match. That means that she has to wait, and hope, for an unrelated donor to come forward.

'It's weird,' says Sian. 'I don't know how long I will live, or how successful my treatment is going to be, but since my diagnosis I am the happiest I have ever been and value every moment. I feel really sad for people who go through life without realizing what is *not* important, and most significantly what *is* important.'

Sian has chosen to channel her surplus energies into helping the Anthony Nolan Trust, an organization that maintains the register of potential bone marrow donors in the UK. Her mission – to spread the word about bone marrow donation and to hopefully help save people in a similar position to her. In only four months she has run a donor recruitment clinic where over 100 people signed up as potential donors.[1] Her next venture is to organize a London Marathon team to raise funds for the Trust, which she will be running in herself. (Gulp!)

As a result of her illness, Sian has learned to live and love her life, however much of it there is still to come. 'My wish is that other people could open their eyes and see how lucky we all are to be alive, and not to waste time by forever striving for things that really aren't that important in the bigger picture of life.'

There are many times in our life where we are faced with a challenge. And we always have a choice: to step up and meet it head on, or pass it over, or even let it overwhelm and consume us. But sometimes there are things in life you simply have to deal with in the moment. Because sometimes, there just isn't another day.

The aim of today is to get really clear on what your challenge is, who it's calling you to become, why you're feeling afraid and what choices you've got. By the end of today, be ready to make a commitment one way or another; a firm decision about your way forward. That'll be your first Gulp!

The Price of Denial

Change itself can be really uncomfortable; that's why we can spend a lot of time in denial avoiding the issue, deflecting it, pretending it doesn't exist, blaming it on someone else. By avoiding the issue we don't have to deal with the pain we think we'll have to go through to get to the outcome. Keep denying it, and it'll build up over time, often turning around to bite you on the bottom when you least expect it.

Take Bob, for example. Bob always wanted to be an accountant. He'd been studying seriously for his accountancy exams and finally passed them all. But once he was there, it was a different story. 'I knew the environment of accountancy was killing me emotionally,' recalls Bob. 'But I was so hooked up on how hard I'd worked to pass the exams. I didn't want to waste all that time. So I kept ignoring my feelings.' In the end his body started to speak for itself, and he developed all kinds of strange stress-related symptoms. Bob knew then that if he didn't leave, his health would really suffer.

The price of denial is high. It comes in the form of suffering, stuckness and sickness.

A: Suffering

We've all experienced those heartfelt moments of deep disappointment when breaking up with a loved one, or deep sorrow when someone close passes away, or deep regret when we let an important opportunity go by. But as we know, time passes and we eventually move on. The question is, how much time do you want to spend suffering? How much time do you want to spend carrying the emotional pain around with you? And what is it doing to you and your relationships, your health and your work?

George Eliot says, '*Deep unspeakable suffering may well be called a "baptism", a regeneration, the initiation into a new state.*' That's because suffering *can* be overcome. Sometimes it provides a much needed catalyst to create important changes in your life. Other times you need to be with the suffering and allow time for the healing process to take place. But the important thing is not to identify with the suffering itself, but rather to see it as a sign that something needs to change. In his book *Universal Compassion*,[2] Geshe Kelsang Gyatso, an internationally renowned teacher of Buddhism, writes, '*If the roof of our house is leaking and the water is dripping through the ceiling, we do not sit back and do nothing. We try to find the hole and mend it. Similarly with suffering, rather than be preoccupied with the suffering itself, we should apply the solution.*'

And it is through being with our suffering and moving through it that we dig deep, and find inner resources and an inner strength we didn't even know we possessed.

Gulp! Reflection

If you are suffering right now, where is your focus?

- Are you focused on the pain of your suffering?
- Or are you focused on finding a solution to your suffering?
- And how long do you choose to suffer for?

B: Stuckness

For me, feeling stuck is one of the worst feelings in the world. I find it totally exasperating. It's like getting a car stuck in the mud and not having enough traction to get it out again. So the wheels just keep spinning, sinking deeper and deeper and throwing mud back into your face. And there seems to be no way out. Being stuck is like a stalemate. You want to move forward, but you fear letting go of what you've got. So you stay where you are. Then you start to get frustrated with yourself. You wind yourself up. You berate yourself for not being stronger, smarter or speedier. This further feeds your frustration. And so it spirals downward. But being stuck doesn't have to be a big issue. Often it means you're in a holding pattern, and you need to evaluate what you want, what you don't want and how you can move forward. The problem comes when you focus on the frustration of stuckness, rather than the evaluation of it and the important signals it sends. As Robert M. Pirsig wrote in the epic classic '*Zen and the Art of Motorcycle Maintenance*',[3] '*Stuckness shouldn't be avoided. It's the psychic predecessor of all real understanding. An egoless acceptance of stuckness is a key to an understanding of all Quality, in mechanical work as in other endeavours.*'

Gulp! Reflection

If you are feeling stuck right now, where is your focus?

- Are you focused on the frustration of your stuckness?
- Or are you focused on what your stuckness is telling you?
- And how long do you choose to stay stuck for?

C: Sickness

I'll never forget the first time I read Louise Hay's book, *You Can Heal Your Life*,[4] where she introduces the concept that 'dis-ease' in your life can manifest itself as illness in your body. She writes on page 123, '*The body, like everything else in life, is a mirror of our inner thoughts and beliefs. Every cell within your body responds to every single thought you think and every word you speak.*' The accumulation of negative thoughts and beliefs and stored emotions like anger, jealousy, fear and hatred can lead to disease appearing in different parts of your body depending on the negative pattern you're holding. Whether you believe this or not, what we all know is that when we're stuck and suffering, invariably we do get run down and we do end up getting sick. In Bob's case, he knew that accountancy wasn't for him, but he stuck it out because he didn't want to waste all the hard work he'd put in. It wasn't until his health began to suffer that he knew he had to do something. What also happens is that as the stress of your situation builds up, it diminishes your ability to cope in the first place.

Gulp! Reflection

If you are feeling run down right now:

- What messages is your body sending you?
- What will happen if you get ill?
- When will you start to do something about your health?

Mirror, Mirror on the Wall

Behind every Gulp! there is a motivator, an internal driver that gives us the energy to move forward. More often than not the pain of our current situation becomes so great that we *just have to do something*. So we are motivated by the necessity to move away from the pain. Other times, it is the thought of the pleasure that awaits us on the other side that becomes the primary motivator. Whatever the situation, we are all motivated by moving towards pleasure or moving away from pain. Interestingly, scientific research has shown that people are more motivated by pain than by pleasure. In fact one study showed that pain is two and a half times more of a motivator than pleasure.

So let's take a moment to look at the pain.

It's clear that you feel some fear about your impending Gulp! and that your current situation is causing you some pain or suffering, otherwise you wouldn't be reading this book. That's because the Gulp! you're facing right now is challenging you. It is bringing to the surface your insecurities, fears and anxieties. Self-awareness is a powerful teacher. It opens your eyes and takes away the shutters so that you view yourself and the world differently. Once you've opened up, it's difficult to close again. As Dr Wayne Dyer says in his book *Everyday Wisdom*,[5] '*When you squeeze an orange, you get orange juice because that's what's inside. The very same principle is true about you. When someone squeezes you – puts pressure on you – what comes out is what's inside.'*

Having coached hundreds of people over the past years, I can say with my hand on my heart that the biggest thing holding you back right now is *you*. Deep down, you know that too. It's easy to look outside and blame the people around you, or the circumstances around you or even the objects around you. That's why we're going to take a good hard look in the mirror and see how *you* are contributing to your own pain and suffering. And when you boil it all down, I bet that the root of your pain will fall into one or more of the following categories.

1. Your needs
2. Your identity
3. Your attachment
4. Your values
5. Your impact

So let's look at each one of these in more detail.

Your Needs

In 1943, Dr Abraham Maslow[6] published his theory on human motivation and hypothesized that we have five levels of needs – Physiological, Safety, Social, Esteem and Self-Actualization. Suffering comes when one of these needs is lacking, being threatened or not being satisfied. Pleasure comes when there is an abundance, where your needs are well and truly being satisfied. In theory, the lower level needs have to be satisfied before we can move up the pyramid. The hungry artist with no money to pay for brushes and paints may not be in the best space to do their most creative and inspiring work. Or the globetrotting couple who relish the adventure of living in third world countries may not be in the best space to start a family. Yet it must be said that this is a dynamic hierarchy and your dominant needs will vary depending on where you are in your life.

Maslow's Hierarchy of Needs

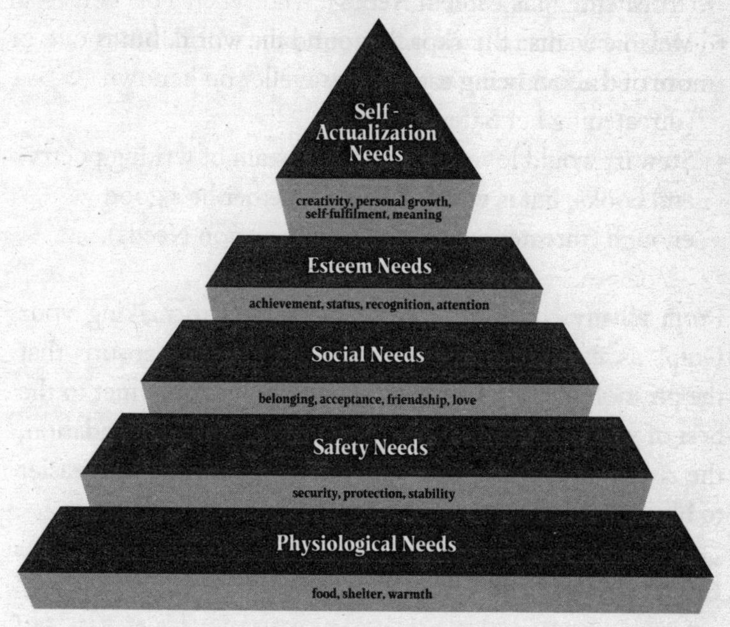

As you step up to your challenge, any changes you make may cause a positive or negative impact to one or more of these levels of needs. If the threat to one need is greater than the pleasure gained by meeting another need, then fear will kick in.

- Simon wants to start his own business and be his own boss, but is worried about the financial impact and whether he can pay the mortgage (threatening his Physiological Needs).
- Paula would love to pack up and go to live in South Africa, but she's worried about not knowing anyone and having to start all over again (threatening her Social Needs).
- Pete's thinking of crossing over to head another department responsible for innovation in his company, but he's worried about losing his profile and influence (threatening his Esteem Needs).
- Melanie wants to backpack around the world, but is worried about being a woman traveller on her own (threatening her Safety Needs).
- Stewart would love to pursue his dream of writing poetry and books, but is worried about whether he's good enough (threatening his Self-Actualization Needs).

From all my coaching, one of the secrets to making your Gulp! as easy and painless as possible is to ensure that the physiological, safety and belonging needs are met to the best of your ability. From there, you form a firm foundation, the risk is lower and you will find it much freer and easier to blossom.

Gulp! Reflection

As you step up to the challenge and start to make changes:

- What needs are being threatened?
- What needs would be more satisfied by making the change?
- What motivates you the most?

Your Identity

'*I am*' many things. I am a woman. I am a Kiwi. I am a writer. I am thirty-something soon to be forty-something. I am an Aries. And the list of my *identities* goes on. But the truth of it is that I am in fact none of these. They are just words. I am me. I am not my identities. My identities are simply labels that help me sort and categorize myself to help me find my place in the world, and help others to do the same. And so we create structures for our world. And so we put ourselves into little boxes with lovely ribbons and bright bows.

We are *not* our identities. Yet one of the biggest stumbling blocks is that stepping up to your Gulp! will mean that you have to let go of one of your identities. Take job titles as a great example. When I used to work as a European Marketing Director for a recognized company, with a nice big leather chair, it was a very grand title that used to open doors for me. But then I set up my own little company. And I always remember the first prospective phone call I made because it completely flummoxed me. I immediately started to say, 'Hi I'm Gabriella Goddard, I am the Eur . . .' And then it struck me. I was no longer this fancy title any more. I was little no-name, from little no-name company. It felt like the big mother ship that had always been behind me was no longer there. I didn't know who I was any more.

Then of course there are all the excuses I make up. For example, I'm great at starting projects but have trouble seeing them through to the end, but that's because *I am an Aries*, so what do you expect? And I could never possibly have a dog in the house, because *I am a cat lover*.

So my life becomes defined by what I am and what I am not. But these categories actually don't exist. We make them up to help us make sense of our world and see where we fit in. But in doing so, we cut off opportunities to grow and change because we get 'stuck' in our identities. We identify with our own identities. The same identity that categorizes us can turn around and box us in and hinder our growth. Once we become that identity, people expect us to behave in a particular way, and more often than not, we expect ourselves to behave in a certain way. And when we break the mould it can create real havoc both for ourselves (in the form of an identity crisis) and for others too.

When it comes to facing your Gulp! you might just find that one of the biggest obstacles stems from your own identity, from both the perspective of the inner crisis this might cause you and the impact that a change will have on other people.

- Karen would like to leave her adulterous husband. But to do that she will have to let go of being 'the Mayor's wife' and all the perks that go with it.
- Robert wants to take a six-month sabbatical and buy a leather jacket and a Harley Davidson and then tour Europe. But he will have to let go of being the serious pin-striped 'Accountant' who 'just doesn't do that sort of thing', and all the credibility that goes with it.
- Deana would like to tell her parents about her accidental pregnancy, but she will have to let go of always being the 'sensible one' in the family and face her parents' disappointment.

So when it comes to facing your Gulp!, think about how you are being boxed in and limited by an identity label. And then eliminate this label. Change the way you phrase who you are, so that you are not associating yourself with a particular identity. Trust me, it can be a truly liberating experience.

For example:

I am a Kiwi	*I was born and bred in New Zealand*
I am a writer	*I write books and articles*
I am an accountant	*I work for an accountancy firm*
I am the black sheep	*I always challenge the family norms*
I am a cat lover	*I love cats*
I am the sensible one	*I tend to be dependable and reliable*
I am a victim	*I feel overwhelmed by my current situation*

Gulp! Reflection

As you step up to your Gulp!:

- Make a list of all the 'I am's that are being challenged by your Gulp!
- What identities will you need to let go of?
- What does it feel like to let these go?
- How can you rephrase this identity so it's no longer an identity, but rather an *identifier*?

Your Attachment

We all get attached to things. We get attached to people (nothing like a broken heart to prove that one). We get attached to objects (as any BlackBerry user will tell you). We get attached to symbols (ever seen more flags than at a football match?). We get attached to emotions (like that ever-present guilt that comes from eating chocolate). We get attached to places (like your favourite little café). And we get attached to outcomes (like being right all the time).

In a similar way to identity, we become attached to our attachments. They start to define us and tie us in to being a certain way. That's who we expect ourselves to be, and what others expect us to be too.

And so our attachments can start to run our life.

- Paul knew that Kate wasn't the right woman for him. She ridiculed him in front of her friends. She wasn't good for him, but he loved her and as much as he tried, he just couldn't let her go.
- Elaine was devastated when she didn't get pregnant right away. Being a career woman she was used to setting goals and always achieved them. This time around though, she had to let go of her expectations of success.
- When Anita left her job to set up her own business, one of her biggest heartbreaks was having to return the company car, a feisty little convertible number. She had to let go of this status symbol and settle for a little runaround.

Gulp! Wisdom

Cling to nothing. Crave for nothing.

Baizhang, Zen Master

Gulp! Time

Gulp! Reflection

Think about your Gulp!

- What are you attached to or clinging on to?
- How do these attachments hold you back?
- What does it feel like to consider letting these attachments go?
- What needs to be in place for you to let go of them?

Your Values

Louisa knew what was going on in the company she worked for, but she didn't say anything to anyone. But as each day went by she became more and more riddled with guilt, and it was starting to take a toll on her health. It wasn't that what they were doing was illegal, but it was underhand, saying one thing and doing another. And if the company was found out, then the implications could be drastic. Louisa kept her mouth shut. But it kept niggling in the back of her mind. Not that she could do anything about it, but it really grated on her to see the boss charming all the staff at their monthly meetings, when really all the time he was plotting their demise. He would of course gain millions from the deal, but what about all the people who had worked hard for him to create such a successful company? What about their job prospects and their financial commitments in this flailing economic environment? It made her physically sick just thinking about it.

For Louisa, her core values were honesty, respect and integrity. What was happening in the company was totally out of alignment with these values. As a result, this made her feel physically ill.

Our values are those fundamental beliefs that form the cornerstones and foundations of our life. They are heavily influenced by our family upbringing and the culture we were brought up in. And as we get older we build our own set of core values based on our experience and what feels right. Because values lie at the core of who we are, when we do something or experience something that is not in alignment with them, we feel out of sync and this makes us feel bad. Keep going against your values and you might start to feel physically ill, because you are acting so contrarily to what you fundamentally believe in.

In Louisa's case, the situation she was in was going completely against her values of honesty, respect and integrity. And while she could manage it for a while, the constant exposure day in and day out was building up to a pivot point, where she could no longer tolerate being so totally out of sync with her true nature. In other instances, you can be pulled towards becoming more aligned to a particular value. Anita really valued 'freedom and choice', and being stuck in her nine-to-five job felt like a prison. So when she left to set up her own business and be her own boss (with her own schedule), she was so much happier because of the freedom and choice this gave her.

As you face your Gulp!, some of the pain you feel may come from one of your core values being compromised. Or it could be that it's time to step up and embrace one of your buried core values more fully.

Gulp! Reflection

Think about your Gulp!

- What core values are being compromised?
- What values are you not honouring?
- What values would you like to honour more?

Your Impact

Making any change in your life is like dropping a pebble in a pond. We are all part of the same natural ecosystem, so when *we* change, things around us have to change as well. That's because when *we* change it changes who we're being, how we're feeling, how we're behaving, what we're thinking, what we're saying and what we're doing. The dynamic of any relationship, whether it is with yourself, with others or even with your environment, is like a dance. Imagine for a moment that you are dancing salsa, the sultry music playing softly in the background. As you step forward on your right foot, your partner naturally steps back. Then when they step forward, you naturally step backwards. And when your partner lifts their arm, you follow the signal and do a feisty double twirl. Well, that's how it's meant to happen anyway. What happens, though, when you step forward with your right foot, but your partner stays still and doesn't move back? Usually an 'ouch' ensues. And what happens when your partner lifts their arm as a signal to twirl and you stay static? You both miss the beat and lose the rhythm of the foot work.

Stepping up to your Gulp! will definitely have a ripple effect. It will change you. It will change the dynamics you have with the people around you. It will change how you are dancing, and this might put your relationships out of sync. It will also change how you feel about your current environment. And it may very well rock the boat, and cause a stir.

When Karl missed out on the promotion he was expecting, it was like a wake-up call. Married with two small children, with another on the way, his life had become like a canned beans production line. Waking at five am every morning to catch the six am train into London so that he could be at the office by eight am, his day didn't stop until twelve hours later when he slumped exhaustedly into the train seat on his one-and-a-half-hour journey home. His contact with his children was pretty much limited to kissing sleeping heads morning and night, and the weekends when, if the truth be known, he felt too exhausted to really engage with them. His marriage was strong, but he sensed that cracks were opening up as his wife did her best to cope with her blossoming pregnancy and managing two children under five. When he got the news about his promotion, something inside him flipped. His journey home was a nightmare due to snow on the line (dare we say the wrong kind of snow?), and it just brought it all home to him. He asked himself, 'Is this what my life is all about? Is this what it's going to be like for the next ten years?' For Karl it was a pivot point. When he arrived home he sat down with his wife and told her the news, the disappointment etched deeply on his face. And that's when he told her that he couldn't go on like this any more. That life had lost its meaning. That working like this day in and day out was killing his spirit. He felt guilty that he wasn't at home more to help her and to spend quality time with the kids. And at the same time he felt guilty that he wasn't putting in the weekend hours that his single colleagues seemed to be able to do, and maybe that's why he missed out on the promotion. It was pulling him apart and he wanted it to stop. But he couldn't see a way out. His outburst opened the floodgates. For the first time in ages, Karl and his wife sat down and talked about their life, where they'd come from and where they were heading. Tears were shed. Fists were pounded on the table. And large pots of tea were drunk. The solution they kept coming back to was to downsize and move to the countryside where Karl could work from home as a consultant. When he looked at the impact of this decision, while he knew that he would be so much happier spending more time with his family and not having to do that horrendous commute five days a week, he worried about losing his regular salary, especially with a baby on the way. Part of him also worried about the gap that this would create in his CV, and whether he would shoot himself in the foot professionally. Despite all this, he knew that his wife and children would be a lot happier that he would see them more and have a more active role in their life, sharing the workload. And he would be so much happier. This could only improve the family environment, and maybe some of the odd jobs he kept promising to get on to around the house would finally get done. His promotion, or rather lack of it, had really been a catalyst for highlighting what was truly important in his life. It was a real wake-up call.

As you step up to your Gulp!, there will be an impact on you, on others and often on the environment around you. It is well worth having a good look at what this impact could be now, because one of your biggest stumbling blocks might boil down to the impact that you will have on those around you, and how you might *feel* about it:

- **Guilty:** Do you feel guilty in any way? That this will make you happier? That others might suffer as a result? That you might get what you want? That others will get angry or upset? Or that they will be disappointed?
- **Responsible:** Do you feel responsible for the people around you in any way? Do you feel that you need to protect them? And if you take this Gulp!, will it leave them exposed? Do you feel responsible for their well-being, their happiness or their safety?
- **Afraid:** Do you feel afraid of the impact that your decision will have on others? Do you fear that your world will fall apart? That you'll lose your security? That others might get angry and retaliate? Are you scared of who you might become, and the changes that this Gulp! will have on you?

We'll talk more about fear in the next chapter, but know that these emotions are low-level feelings and real inhibitors to you moving forward. Right now, the focus is on expanding your awareness – being aware of the impact your Gulp! will have on you, on others and on your environment, and understanding the feelings that you associate with this impact.

Gulp! Reflection

Think about your Gulp!

- If you step up to it, what impact will it have on:
    1. You?
    2. Others?
    3. Your Environment?
- What negative feelings does this bring up?
- What positive feelings does this bring up?

Discover the Silver Lining

'Everything can be taken from a man or a woman but one thing: the last of human freedoms to choose one's attitude in any given set of circumstances, to choose one's own way,' said Dr Viktor Frankl, a survivor of the Nazi concentration camps. His book *Man's Search for Meaning*[7] is an autobiography about the three years he endured in the camps where his father, mother, brother and wife all perished. Despite the hardship, misery and despair he so clearly suffered, he brings a real message of hope; that even in the midst of suffering, a person can find meaning.

Every cloud has a silver lining, as alluded to by the seventeenth-century poet John Milton, in the masque 'Comus', which he wrote for the Earl of Bridgewater.

Gulp! Wisdom

Was I deceiv'd, or did a sable cloud
turn forth her silver lining on the night?
John Milton

Gulp! Time

The 'silver lining' is thought to refer to the edge of a cloud that appears to glow when rays of sunlight shine brightly from behind it; a metaphor to suggest that inherent in all perceived darkness and negativity there is something useful and positive.

In the same way, the challenge you are facing has a silver lining. It will stretch and test you. It will dare and defy you.

And it will make your heart beat faster and might even scare the pants off you.

So where is the silver lining in that, I hear you ask?

Stepping up to the challenge and making breakthroughs in your life is the perfect antidote to mediocrity. We get too comfortable in our lives. We don't want to rock the boat. We'd rather suffer in silence than claim the full life that is rightfully ours. When I look at the world today, I see a place of immense opportunity and possibility. Yet why are so many of us stuck in our lives, trapped by fear and scarcity. I do believe that the government and the media have a lot to answer for regarding the latter. Just watching the news of an evening can be enough to make you not want to set foot outside the safety of your own home.

Clare had reached a crisis point. She worked for a large organization, putting her heart and soul into her job. She loved it and worked ten hour days. She had a team of ten young and committed people who always went the extra mile for her. One day, she was told that there would be a review of her team structure. Running parallel with this were two other challenges. First, she'd just bought her first flat which needed a lot of DIY. Secondly, her boyfriend was becoming emotionally abusive and very unsupportive. Clare felt like she was trapped on a rollercoaster and didn't know how to get off.

Then, on a skiing trip, she remembered how much she wanted to go to Australia. Because of her age, she had only a few more months to submit a working holiday application. On a complete whim, she went ahead and applied. When she returned to work, she was told that two of her team members were going to be made redundant. Worse still, she wasn't going to be allowed to be there to support them when they were told. Clare was furious. It was the straw that broke the camel's back. 'I asked myself, "what's it all for?" ' recalls Clare. 'And then something in me flipped and I made a decision, not knowing quite how to go ahead. I just had to make a stand for myself.'

At lunchtime, she booked a flight to Australia, and then went back to work and resigned. She had just twelve weeks to leave her job, rent out the flat, ditch her boyfriend and hand over her job to the remaining team. 'Australia changed my life,' says Clare. 'I learned about me, my relationships and my career. In one year I was redefined and clear about how I want to live. I couldn't be more certain.' Looking back, Clare says that the silver lining in her challenge was the realization that no-one controls what you do unless you let them and that you can travel or run away but you always come back to yourself. Making a stand was scary, but it was also fun and empowering. And she also learnt that you don't need to know the big master plan. She says, 'Just have a plan to get to the next stage and trust that you'll figure it out when you get there.'

We all live in a world of immense possibility of our own creating, yet often we do little to actually enjoy or take advantage of it. Many of us are trapped in the prisons of our own minds, where fear and failure play out in full technicolour. We are bound by the 'shoulds' and 'oughts' that society places on us and by the family ties, financial ties and loyalty ties from which there seems to be no exit. Our lives are shrinking. Where has our sense of risk and adventure gone? Where has the pioneering spirit of our ancestors disappeared to? We have become too comfortable, too stuck and too limited in our thinking. And worst of all – we don't even realize it because we are 'in' our lives.

We can only change this by changing ourselves. And this starts with changing our awareness. Like Clare, when we step out of our comfort zone, we expand our awareness of what 'could be'. We open up to new opportunities, new possibilities and new dimensions. We become new versions of ourselves. We think differently, we believe differently and we act differently. We discover qualities about ourselves and a resolve that we didn't even know existed. This takes our life down a different trajectory. From this new place we can create again, and again, and again. And so we grow and evolve as individuals; and so society grows and evolves as a collective. And with that emerge new leaders, new thinking, new inventions, new breakthroughs and the shape of a new world consciousness.

It is difficult to do this all from a place of stuckness! When you answer the call of your Gulp!, the silver lining is that you are saying 'no' to mediocrity and 'yes' to a life that grows and evolves you. Don't be afraid. Challenges are good. Challenges are the catalyst for breakthrough. And breakthroughs are the essence of your, and our, collective evolution.

Whatever situation you're facing, it is a call to action. It is a call to confront something head on that will teach you valuable lessons about yourself. And it is a call to say, 'it's time to make a breakthrough.' You know it, and I know it.

What's more, you DO have what it takes. And you WILL find a way through it.

Gulp! Reflection

As you face your Gulp!:

- What will the experience teach you?
- What difference will it make if you are successful?
- What three personal qualities or virtues will you need to draw on?

Naming the Challenge

Gulp! Wisdom

In the face of challenge,
Who do you choose to be?
The one who stalls and stagnates,
Or the one who flies free?

Gulp! Time

One of the simplest and most powerful ways of snapping yourself out of denial is to face your challenge head on and name it. When you name something, you have to deal with it. Instead of some whimsical thought dancing about in your mind, it becomes a real, live and tangible thing. It also means that once you've named it, you're forced to do something about it.

'I remember sitting on my bed one morning after months of suffering, wondering how to get through the day,' recalls Edna, 'and found myself saying, "You must go in and through." That's when I knew that I had to take charge of my situation, rather than continue to be overwhelmed by it.' Edna was on the brink of forty, professionally successful and personally in very good shape, happy, surrounded by wonderful friends, fit as a fiddle and fully engaged in a very interesting profession. But suddenly, everything started to tumble around her. Three of her most beloved friends had died and her mother had begun the inexorable and horrible slide into Alzheimer's. To make matters worse, Edna even got two major sports injuries, both in the same leg, which put paid to the relief and pleasure of tennis and badminton and brought home the pain of limitation. Life took her over. She walked around like a zombie, only just functioning and attending her first funerals. 'Over a period of about three years, I began to understand how deeply grief penetrates your very bones, and how it returns and returns until one is grieving for much more than a lost loved one; one grieves also for the first major cracks in confidence, for beliefs which had kept a semblance of safety until then, for being spun out into uncertainty and for this new and shocking experience of life going down as well as up,' says Edna.

But three years later, the moment when she was sitting on her bed that morning wondering how to get through the day was a pivot point. Saying the words, 'you must go in and through', was like a jolt, a wake-up call. And from there, things started to change for the better. She began to listen to what this whole experience was teaching her. She started to say 'yes' and 'thank you' to what life brought her. She realized that joy includes sadness, that light and dark go together and that the whole experience was a powerful learning. 'Death is a very painful teacher and I don't like it,' says Edna. 'But I've come to see how it can lead to the marriage of mind and heart and to the gradual trust in the extraordinary processes of Life itself.'

Naming your challenge makes it real. It brings it into reality. And that means you can, or rather have to, do something about it.

Gulp! Reflection

Think about the Gulp! you're facing:

- Write down what your challenge is in *one sentence*.
- How does it make you feel?

The Pivot Point

By now you understand the deeper meaning and what breakthrough your Gulp! is calling you to make. We've explored your pain and the attachments that might be holding you back. We've evaluated your internal drivers and the impact they may have on you, on others and on your environment. And now you've named your challenge.

You have reached the 'pivot point'.

It's now time to make a choice. So what are you going to do? This is always an interesting one. We all have free will, free choice. We can choose our response to any situation and we can make the choice about what action we will take. Even in the most miserable of times, we still have choice.

Take falling in love, for example. She fell in love with him the moment he sat next to her at a friend's dinner party. The problem was he was married and so was she. The passion was reciprocal and they met only once to discuss the spark between them. The two choices they had were not acceptable to either of them. But they continued as friends and their families became close over the years with everything between them totally above board. That was, until seven years later. One day he called her and asked her to meet him. With her heart in her mouth, she joined him, expecting the ultimatum: 'We've only got one life,' etc. But she was dumbfounded when he told her that he and his wife had decided to go and live in New Zealand. She was heartbroken. She saw them off at Heathrow with a heavy heart. After that, there was little news of them. Just the occasional long newsy letter at Christmas. So she got on with her life and her family. Then, fifteen years later, there was no Christmas letter. She waited as long as she could, but one day could bear it no longer. With her heart in her mouth, she called him. Then, a few days later she received a long letter from him in the post with bitter sweet news. His wife had left him eighteen months earlier. But that was not all. He had been diagnosed with Motor Neurone Disease. She was devastated. He was dying. It had taken twenty years, but finally she'd reached her 'pivot point'. Within three days she was on a plane to New Zealand. 'There are some things in life you simply have to do, and this was one of them,' she recalls. 'At the risk of destroying my marriage and alienating my grown children, I had to go.' She was completely honest with her family and made it quite clear that if they didn't want her back, then she'd be heartbroken but that she'd understand. In New Zealand she shared a wonderful six weeks with him. When she left, she knew that she was leaving him to get on with the 'job' of dying. In fact his last words to her were, 'My timing is awful isn't it? The first time we met we were both married, now I'm dying.' He passed away shortly afterwards. Nowadays, whenever she's confronted by a challenge, she remembers him and the immense courage it took for her to actually get on that plane. 'It was such a leap of faith into the dark, trusting the feelings that had surfaced more than twenty years ago. But it was something I just knew I had to do,' she says softly.

The message here is that whatever Gulp! you are facing, you have a choice. You can choose your attitude towards it. You can choose how you feel about it. You can choose the spectacles through which you view it. You can choose the path you take. And you can choose when to step up. But sometimes, there isn't another day. Sometimes there are things in life that you simply have to do.

And if not now . . . when?

So let's look at some of the choices you could make:

Give Up

Yes, you could simply close this book right now and never think about it again. But I bet that much as you might want to give up, there's that niggling sense of 'what if' and 'just suppose' in the back of your mind. That's because deep down you know it's time to step up.

Give An Inch

Okay, so you're not prepared to give up completely. You're thinking about it. You're testing the waters. You're open to chew over the option of maybe, just possibly, you might do something about it. But you're still not going to commit just yet.

Give A Mile

You're ready to commit. You're going to say 'yes' to this challenge, and you're going to give it your best shot. You're going to step up to the plate and bite the bullet.

Okay, so you get a few flutters in the stomach at the mere thought of it, but hey, who doesn't? And underneath all those flutters, I bet there is the sweet taste of anticipation and, dare I say it, excitement.

Give It All

You're feeling radical. You're truly sick and tired of the way things are. You want change, and you want it now. You want to say 'no' to mediocrity. You've been there for too long, done that and got the T-shirt. And you want to say 'yes' to living a full and vibrant life; one that makes your heart sing and your soul dance. It's time to embrace risk and radical change.

Gulp! Wisdom

The choice of truth is here to make.
It's up to you, which path you take.

Gulp! Time

We are at the 'pivot point'. Which choice are you going to make? Are you going to sit in the middle and simply dip your toe in the water? Or are you going to throw caution to the wind and jump into the unknown, and see where that takes you?

Note that there is never a 'right' or 'wrong' choice. There's just the choice you decide to make. Although could I make a small request here? Dare to think big. Dare to raise the bar. Dare to be radical. And trust that you are much stronger and more capable than even you dare to think you are!

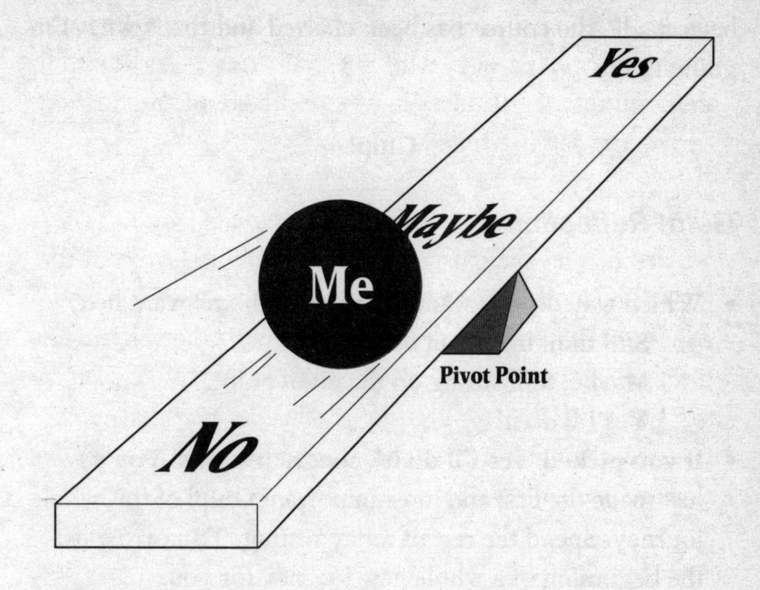

In my research with people who have made major breakthroughs in their lives, there is always a defining moment; an epiphany; a point at which a conscious decision is made. Something 'flips' or just 'clicks' into place. For me, there is almost a physical 'click' sound, like the gears shifting on a bicycle. Thinking back to past Gulps! – sometimes the trigger for moving past the 'pivot point' has been a throw-away comment, or an article I've read in a newspaper, or something really simple (usually annoying) that has happened to me that day. And in that moment, something just clicks into place. It's hard to describe. But I'm sure you know exactly what I mean. There's a distinct shift in energy. It's like the last piece of a jigsaw puzzle that clicks into place to complete the picture. At that point, my choice and my decision become crystal clear. What's more, there is a feeling of dead certainty, a feeling of no going back. But funnily enough, that doesn't frighten me. It's like the decision has been made, the course has been charted and that's what I'm going to do.

Gulp!

Gulp! Reflection

- Which way do you want to tip? (tick the relevant box)
  - ☐ Still thinking about it.
  - ☐ Maybe. Still sitting on the pivot point.
  - ☐ Yes I'll do it!
- **If you picked 'yes I'll do it'**, congratulations! You've just made the first and most important Gulp! of this whole journey. Spend the rest of today resting. Tomorrow is the beginning of a whole new journey for you.
- **If you picked 'maybe'**, you're really really close, so what is the missing piece? Make a list of what you need to know, hear, feel or see to tip you over to committing. Your mission today is to find out, and sort out, each one. No more procrastination. Nut it on the head, right now.
- **If you picked 'still thinking about it'**, I want you to be really honest with yourself. Remember, all you need to do at this point is make the conscious choice that you will step up to your Gulp!. You don't have to say *how* you're going to do it yet. That comes later. So write down in your journal what else you need to know, hear, feel or see before you'll commit to the challenge. If there really is no tipping you over right now, then I recommend you work through the rest of the book and set the intention that by the end, you will be ready and able to make the conscious decision and be able to tick the 'yes I'll do it' box.

Gulp! Day 1 Summary: Dare & Defy

The five things to remember:

1. Name the challenge. Writing it down makes it real.
2. Every challenge has a silver lining. What will yours teach you?
3. Find out what's at the core of your suffering – fear or pain? What is being threatened? What are you too attached to?
4. Tip past the 'pivot point'. Make the conscious decision to commit to your challenge. Do it today. Do it now.
5. Be daring. You can choose to play safe and inch forward, or you can stretch right outside your comfort zone and make a quantum leap. Which would you prefer?

Gulp! Action Plan: Dare & Defy

I ______________________ [insert name] commit to:

____

____

____

____

The three things that scare me the most are:

1. ____
2. ____
3. ____

The challenge will show me and teach me that:

In committing to this challenge I will need to be *more*:

In committing to this challenge I will need to be *less*:

I will know that I've been successful because:

The three things that will keep me motivated through the challenge are:

1.

2.

3.

Gulp! Espresso

Take fifteen minutes right NOW, to complete your Gulp! Action Plan. Make sure you're in a quiet place free from interruptions. Don't think too hard about it. Go with your instincts and write down whatever pops into your head, even if it doesn't make complete sense right now.

Gulp! Mediano

Find a quiet space and spend at least one hour working through the Gulp! Reflection exercises. Write down in your journal all the thoughts that come up for you. When you're ready, extract the most important insights and write them down in the spaces provided in the Gulp! Action Plan above. Make sure that your commitment is clear, concise and challenging enough!

Gulp! Grande

Over the coming week, spend some quiet time each day reflecting upon the contents of this chapter and work through all the Gulp! Reflection exercises. Start with the challenge you're facing and peel back the layers. Write your thoughts down in your journal. Be open minded, because in the process you may find that your original challenge changes, especially if this self-awareness process reveals a more profound challenge lying beneath it. By the end of the week, complete the Gulp! Action Plan. Make a strong and clear commitment. And remember . . . be daring!

Gulp! Wisdom Word

Quieten your mind and think of a number between 1 and 250.

Turn to pages 307–10 and find the word that relates to this number.

What new thoughts does this word spark?

Wisdom Word:

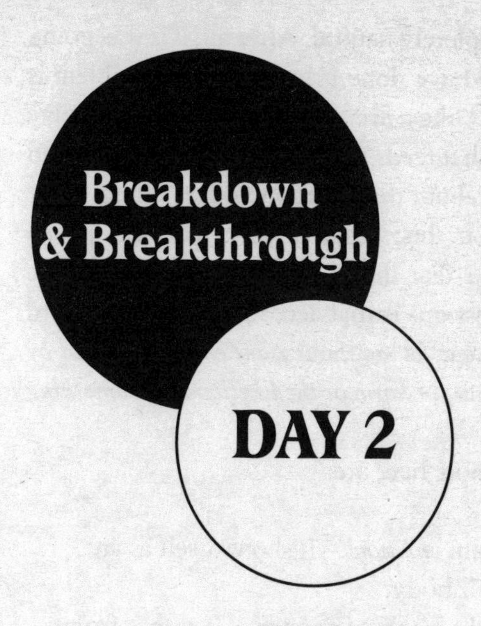

Gulp! Aims For Today

To face your fears.
To understand how fear works.
To break through the fear barrier.

Gulp! Time

Facing your Gulp! means moving outside your comfort zone and into unfamiliar territory. Because it's a new experience, it's hard to predict the outcome. So you start to worry. You start to fret about what might happen or what might go wrong. You fear failure, fear rejection, fear success, fear looking stupid, fear dying, fear being vulnerable, fear being laughed at, fear the unknown . . . and you might even fear

fear itself. This is completely natural. After all, if it was going to be easy you would have done it by now. The problem is that your fear becomes like a fire. The more oxygen you give it the worse it gets. What feeds fear is your attention to it and your fearful thoughts about the situation you're facing.

But let me ask you this; what if your fear was all an illusion? What if your fear didn't need to exist at all? The reason I ask these questions is that according to The Oxford English Dictionary, 'fear' is '*an unpleasant emotion caused by the threat of danger, pain, or harm or the likelihood of something unwelcome happening*.'

The key words to note here are:

- Fear is an 'unpleasant *emotion*' – it shows itself as an emotion felt by your body.
- Fear is caused by 'the *threat* of danger' – it comes from anticipating something unwelcome possibly happening in the future. It's not a sure thing, just a possibility.

So fear, then, is based on a *perceived* possibility of pain happening in the future, based on what you've experienced in the past. It is *not* based on the reality of your current situation. The powerful thing about saying this is that if your fears are based on what you *perceive* might happen, that means you can flip fear by changing your perception. By mastering your mind, you can change the rational and emotional impacts of fear.

And that is the essence of today. YOU create your fear. It doesn't actually exist. You create fear based on your perception of a situation. That means that if you can create your own fear, then you can uncreate it as well. YOU are in charge of your own fear.

What I want you to do today is become an observer of fear and put it under the microscope. Actually, to be frank, I want you to nut it on the head. It's so easy to let your own fear get the better of you and hold you back. But I want you to see it for exactly what it is. See it for what it's telling you. Name it. And ask yourself what you can do about it. Remember, you created it.

To start with we're going to demystify fear and break it down into bite-sized bits. We're going to examine the rational and emotional impact that it can have. We're going to explore the strong mind/body connection that comes with fear. And then we'll look at ways you can break through the fear barrier; proactively manage your fear. To finish off, we'll cover ten powerful strategies that can help you break through fear any time, any place.

By the end of today I want you to feel that YOU are in the driving seat of your own fear. I want you to be confident that you can master fear any time you step up and Gulp!. I want you to understand that your mind creates the fear you're feeling, so your mind can actually undo it as well. Or you can create different strategies to minimize the fear. That's because YOU are the master or mistress of your mind.

An important note here is that if your fear is truly overpowering and overwhelming you might like to seek the help of a professional to assist you in working through it.

Gulp! Wisdom

FEAR =
FALSE
EVIDENCE
APPEARING
REAL
Veer Sharma

Gulp! Time

Facing Your Fear

Sue was a senior manager in the world of internal communications. A natural high achiever, she'd risen quickly through the ranks becoming a Director of Internal Communications for a major telecommunications company by her mid-thirties. But one of Sue's greatest fears was standing up and speaking in public. So when she got the call from a professional association to see if she would be interested in speaking at their annual conference, her stomach somersaulted. 'I'm petrified of public speaking,' recalls Sue. 'I freeze up, I can't breathe and I can't think straight.'

Quite aptly, they'd asked if she could speak on 'crisis communications'. This was a topic she was very familiar with, having managed a number of crises within her current organization. This was one topic that, if she had to speak, would be the one she could manage the best. 'While I felt extremely nervous,' remembers Sue, 'at the same time I had that weird feeling when you're really petrified of doing something, but there's a tiny part of you that thinks,

"I'm really scared, but actually I'd quite like to have a go." '

So she took a Gulp! and said 'Yes!' After all it was the safest subject she could choose. On top of that it was a high profile conference. If it did go well it would really boost her reputation. But if it went badly, well . . . let's not go there.

Once she agreed, she put it to the back of her mind. Then the marketing emails started to come out promoting the conference. Sue was horrified. In the first email to arrive in her inbox, she saw that she was singled out as one of the key speakers. By the final mailing, she was the top speaker for the event. Poor Sue, you can imagine the additional pressure and stress of that!

Her manic work schedule was a blessing in disguise in that it kept her mind off the upcoming conference. Part of her was regretting she'd even agreed to speaking. Then, a few weeks before the conference, she was looking at her diary and saw the date looming before her. And she knew it was time to sit down and start preparing for it. 'When I sat down and started to prepare the slides for the presentation, it became real. And that's when it hit me, and the nerves started bubbling up again,' recollects Sue. Funnily enough, at about the same time she'd been commissioned by a client to create a booklet on communication skills, and one of the sections was top tips for public speaking. Ironically, in writing the booklet, she'd done extensive research on how to deliver winning presentations. 'It made sense then to follow my own hints and tips,' says Sue. 'So in the end I wrote a really good presentation, with all the right ingredients and a good structure. Whatever was going to happen on the day, at least I had got a good structure.' Producing a good set of slides gave Sue a real confidence boost.

But the day before the conference Sue's confidence

plummeted. Her biggest fear was that she'd trip over her words and forget what she was saying. Or worse still, she'd be boring and not connect with the audience at all. She was now deeply regretting agreeing to present at the conference. But being the practical type, Sue made herself a cup of tea, sat down and spent hours going through the presentation in minute detail. 'What finally did it for me was getting the story clear in my head,' recalls Sue. 'Once I had the flow straight and knew exactly what I was going to say for each slide, I knew that if I *did* panic, I'd have enough armour around me to get me through.'

The morning of the conference arrived, and Sue was understandably feeling panicky and hassled. And then, walking to the train station something odd happened. As she neared the top of the street, her eye caught sight of a tree standing tall and calmly, as it had obviously done for decades. Sue laughs, 'As soon as I saw that tree I thought to myself, "I need a bit of that calm!" ' So she stood for a few moments looking at the tree until it became clearly fixed in her mind.

It worked. By the time she arrived at the conference hall she was definitely feeling calmer. She no longer wanted to dwell on the presentation. She was there. She was prepared. And she was ready. But when it was her turn to speak, her stomach lurched again. It was Gulp! time. Her palms felt clammy. She became breathless. But as she walked up to the lectern, she thought about the tree, standing tall and calm. And by the time she showed the first slide, she knew she was going to be okay. The slides were good, she'd practised the presentation so many times and she almost knew it off by heart. Her notes were in front of her and the microphone was working. And so she looked out into the audience and simply imagined she was having a conversation with each person in the room. The more she spoke, the more confident she became, and the more nods of agreement she was seeing (a good sign). As she came off the stage at the end, it was a huge relief. 'It was like I'd just finished an exam. I thought things had gone well, but I wasn't sure until I got the mark of how well I'd done,' remembers Sue. Thankfully, the feedback was excellent, with some saying it was the most inspirational presentation of the day.

Looking back, Sue says 'To be honest, I still don't really like doing presentations. But it was a great learning experience. If they'd cancelled it I would have been really disappointed because despite my initial panic, a little part of me *did* want to give it a shot. And it was a great feeling to remember how petrified I was about it, yet I went out there and did it and did a really good job. Before, giving a presentation at a conference was a thing I couldn't do, or wouldn't do; an unknown challenge that stood in my way. But until I tried it, I never knew whether I could do it or not. I believe that the more you do the things you're scared of, the more you'll learn that you *will* be just fine. In fact, I think it can be much harder when you don't step up to the challenge!'

Sue's biggest fear was that she'd trip over her words and forget what she was saying. Or worse still, that she'd be boring and not connect at all with the audience. Valid concerns, but at the end of the day not strong enough to stop her from stepping up to her Gulp! That's because she named her fears. She knew exactly what the triggers were, and was then able to develop strategies to minimize the risk of them even happening.

This is a great example of someone who faced one of her

deepest fears and stepped up to the challenge. It is incredible how public speaking can be so nerve-racking. Rationally, all you're doing is standing up in front of a group of people and talking through some points in your presentation. So why does it trigger such a dramatic emotional and physiological response for so many millions of people?

What Are You Actually Afraid Of?

Gulp! Wisdom

We do not see things as they are.
We see them as *we* are.
Talmud

Gulp! Time

When fear comes into your life, it is a very powerful teacher. It signals to you that there is an inner shift that needs to be made. And at the moment, the lack of shift is holding you back, holding you small and holding you in a place that breeds discontent. Fear is a powerful sign that you need to address an aspect of yourself. There's a hidden part of you that is being called to come out. Or there's an identity, attachment or need that you have to let go of. In fact we often don't even question who we are being until a fearful situation arises that forces us to look inwards.

As Dorothy Rowe says in *Beyond Fear*[1] (page 55), '*Everyone knows that no two people are the same and no two people see things in the same way. This knowledge not only enables us to see every person as a unique individual, but also to understand that the meaning we give to ourselves and our world is made up of structures which we have created.'*

The reason that you are feeling fear as you face your Gulp! is that some of your 'structures', or the meanings you place on things, are being challenged, and the way in which you see yourself and your life is being questioned. You are having to re-evaluate yourself and the world you live in. That's why you feel afraid. You are questioning the fundamental foundations of your life.

That's why fear is a powerful teacher. It forces you to reassess your beliefs and perceptions. Some of them may have gone past their 'use by' date. Maybe they were important once upon a time, but now they are no longer relevant.

Fear also shows us that it is time to let go of some part of the image that we hold of ourselves. Sue (who happens to be one of the most capable people I know) had to let go of the notion that she was no good at presenting. In fact, when she put her mind to it and prepared well for it, she got feedback to say that she was 'inspiring'. It was the fear that was flung up when she faced her speaking challenge that brought her to the point where she had to reassess and redefine her own image of herself. Having been successful on this first attempt, she has since made other presentations, each time proving to herself that she can stand up in front of a large group and deliver a powerful presentation. Hence her view of herself is slowly changing. And as that changes, she shifts to a different place of her own self-identity. She develops 'new eyes' and naturally starts to see the world in a different light. And as new challenges come her way, they stir up a different fear from within, and each time she needs to redefine who she is and evolve as an individual.

Many of our fears are also ignited by the opinions of others. But remember, their opinions and judgements are born and bred from their own 'structures' and experiences which have been influenced by many factors, not least their upbringing, their culture, their social standing, and the norm in their family. So more often than not, their opinion is not entirely relevant to your situation, from the simple viewpoint that their perspective is different. Note that doesn't make them *wrong*, rather it is a different viewpoint specific to that person's interpretation of the situation.

As you think about your Gulp!, fear will be an instinctive response because you are stepping outside your comfort zone into the unknown, facing an outcome that you might find dangerous and threatening. The degree of fear you feel about it will depend on how much of a threat you 'perceive' the possible outcome to be. This, of course, has been an important factor in our evolution. A split decision coming face to face with a hungry bear can mean the difference between life and death.

So think about your Gulp!. The fear that you are feeling right now holds an important message for you. It shows you that even as you simply think about your Gulp!, you're pre-empting a particular outcome that's not particularly pleasant. That's because it's happened to you, or someone else, in the past. But this is a different time, a different place and a different situation. Will it really happen again? Or could you pre-empt, or even create, a completely different outcome?

Gulp! Reflection

Think about your Gulp! for a moment:

- What are you actually afraid of?
- When has this situation happened before and what was the outcome?
- What fundamental beliefs is it challenging?

Gulp! Wisdom

The satiated man and the hungry one do not see
the same thing when they look upon
a loaf of bread.
Rumi

Gulp! Time

How Does Fear Impact You?

Think of the best outcome for your Gulp! and you'll feel your heart expanding and a smile will light your face. Think of your worst outcome and you'll feel yourself shrinking; your stomach will sink, your breath will quicken and your heart will beat faster.

Try this now.

Isn't it interesting that simply *thinking* about something can create a physiological reaction. This shows how clearly your feelings respond to your thoughts, creating a physiological and measurable response in your body. This is the power of your mind/body connection. And that's before anything has even happened!

Clearly, if you step up to your Gulp! from a place of fearfulness, your view will be narrow, restricted and overly cautious. It can completely cloud how you're seeing the situation. It'll be like looking through binoculars on a misty day with just one eye. When you view your situation from a place of fear, it limits your thinking. It limits the possibilities that you see before you. It throws you off centre and inhibits your ability to respond calmly and rationally to the pressures that inevitably lie before you. And from a physiological perspective your body becomes tight and tense, putting you off centre when the pressure hits.

And this all starts in your mind, triggered by your fearful thoughts of what might possibly happen.

It is an instinctive response to something you consciously or subconsciously *perceive* as a potential threat, whether real or illusory. The key word here though is 'perceive'. When you 'perceive' that your Gulp! will be potentially dangerous to your security and personal well-being, it will trigger an *instinctive fear response* which then triggers physiological changes in your body – whether your rational mind says to or not. That's why it's instinctive. It puts you into 'freeze, fight or flight' mode. Great if you're facing a lion in the jungle, but is it really the space that you want to be in as you face your Gulp!? Because fear starts in your mind, *you already have the power to influence it*. And if you could catch your fear in the moment, you wouldn't create any of these triggers in the first place.

Gulp! Wisdom

When you change your perception
you can disarm the fear trigger.

Gulp! Time

The Cat and the Creak

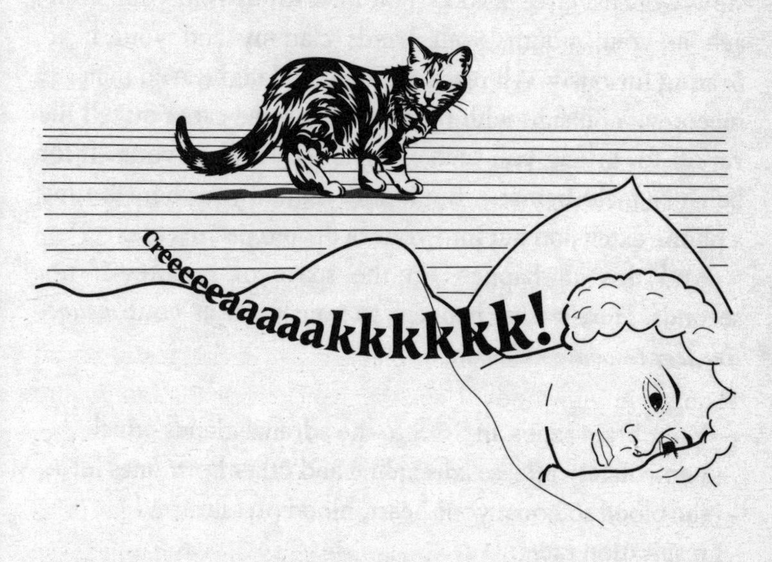

Take the cat and the creak as an example. Just imagine: you're in bed just on the brink of falling asleep and you hear a floorboard creak close by. Creak. Instantly, you freeze. You become alert, and feel the adrenaline pulsing through your veins. Creak. There it is again. Your heart pounds loudly. 'It's just the cat,' you try to tell yourself. Creak. It appears to be coming closer. Your mouth goes dry. You remember the movie you saw yesterday about a family tied and bound and robbed at knife point. You Gulp! 'C'mon, it's just the cat,' you say to yourself, trying to sound convincing. At the same time you're thinking, 'Right, if it is a burglar I'll quickly get out of bed, shut the door, put a chair behind it, and then climb out of the window and run around to the neighbours for help.' Feeling a little better with your plan intact, you listen alertly, ready to act. There's another creak, even closer. Creak. And then it's right outside your door. You hold your breath. Then the door to your bedroom slowly opens. Creeaaakkk. You look towards it, your stomach in your mouth, your hands clammy and your heart beating furiously. All ready for fight and flight. And then . . . meeoow. You sigh with relief. It WAS the cat. You tell the cat off for giving you such a fright and laugh at yourself for being so melodramatic. But it does remind you about getting a phone extension put into your bedroom just in case.

And this all happens in the space of minutes if not seconds. Here's what happens to your body as your *instinctive fear response* kicks in:

- Your brain sends an SOS to the adrenal glands which immediately release adrenaline and other hormones into the blood to boost your heart, blood pressure and respiration rates.
- Your heart beats faster to take more oxygen and nutrients to the body (to prepare you to jump out of bed, shut the door and climb out of the window in record time).
- Your breathing increases to bring more oxygen into your lungs (once you're outside you're going to need to run fast to get to the neighbour's house).
- Your pupils dilate to bring in more light (so that you can see better and more clearly in the dim light).

- Your hearing and sense of smell sharpen to prepare you for a rapid response (helping you to hear each creak and gauge how close they're getting).
- The blood flow to the major muscles in your arms and legs increases (ready for instant action to push the door shut and frighten the burglar if you need to).
- Your liver releases more glucose into the bloodstream to boost your energy reservoir (you've had a hard day and you need all the extra energy you can get).
- Your hands feel clammy and you start to sweat (with all that extra blood flow and energy your body heats up and it's got to vent somewhere).
- Your stomach stops digesting your dinner (this is a state of emergency after all), you feel butterflies in your stomach and your mouth goes dry.
- Your blood supply speeds to the frontal parts of your brain which are responsible for higher levels of reasoning (so that you can make better snap decisions).

This is the amazing ability of your body to respond to a threatening situation. And most of it on the first creak.

This is what happens to your body every time you see the fear in your Gulp! The fearful thoughts trigger this physiological response. And while this adrenaline rush can serve you in some situations, it puts you at the mercy of your instinctive fear responses.

Is this really the space that you want to be in as you step up and Gulp!?

Gulp! Wisdom

Fear makes the wolf bigger than he is.
German Proverb

Gulp! Time

Gulp! Reflection

Think about your Gulp! and imagine the worst case scenario:

- Where do you feel the fear in your body?
- What physiological body symptoms does your fear produce?
- What happens to your body posture?

Fear Starts in the Mind

Gulp! Wisdom

When things go wrong in our life and we encounter difficult situations, we tend to regard the situation itself as the problem.
But in reality, whatever problems we experience come from the mind.
Geshe Kelsang Gyatso

Gulp! Time

I don't know about you, but sometimes I can really frustrate myself by not being able to do something because of the physical 'fear' symptoms that crop up; like breathlessness, heart pounding, dry mouth and words getting stuck in my throat. There are so many times when I let fear stand in my way, both physically and mentally. As much as my mind might be saying what a good idea this Gulp! is, and how it could be easy, enjoyable, exciting, beneficial, etc, my body is reacting in a completely different way – sometimes in a completely irrational way that I don't understand. Yet I can't seem to stop myself. My natural physiological response takes over and I react from a place of fear, often in a knee-jerk way and usually to my detriment. As a result, I Gulp! and mess up.

Learning about the brain has been a huge eye opener for me. It shows me how my brain processes and creates fear, and how I can break the fear circuit. I am in charge of my brain, and with this new awareness I can now use the same processes that created my fear to create a different emotion, like hope or passion or enthusiasm. Now, instead of getting frustrated with myself about my inability to do something that seems rationally quite simple, I'm more self-aware and understanding of what is actually happening *physiologically* to cause me to be this way. I can now catch the physiological feelings of fear in the moment, and choose to let them envelop me, or create space and transform them into something that can actually propel me forward in a positive way.

Gulp! Wisdom

Nothing in life is to be feared.
It is only to be understood.
Marie Curie

Gulp! Time

Let me explain what goes on in your brain when you succumb to fear. Take the case of 'the cat and the creak' for example. Much as your mind was saying, 'It's the cat, it's the cat,' your body didn't believe you, nor did it listen. It reacted instinctively. My own curiosity led me to the work of Joseph Le Doux, the author of *The Emotional Brain*,[2] and the Director at the Center for the Neuroscience of Fear and Anxiety at New York University. He has spent over twenty years researching the cognitive, emotional and motivational functions of the brain, particularly that of fear.

What his work shows is that there are four key bits of the brain at play here:

1. **The Thalamus**: which we'll call 'the router'. This is like a receptor that *receives* all the sensory information coming in (sight, sound, smell, taste, touch) then *routes* it to the *amygdala*, and then to the *neocortex*. It makes no judgement on the sensory information, it just routes it. So the sound of the first creak was picked up by your thalamus which routed the information immediately to your *amygdala* and *neocortex*.
2. **The Amygdala**: which we'll call 'the reactor'. This is an almond-shaped part of the brain that is regarded as the

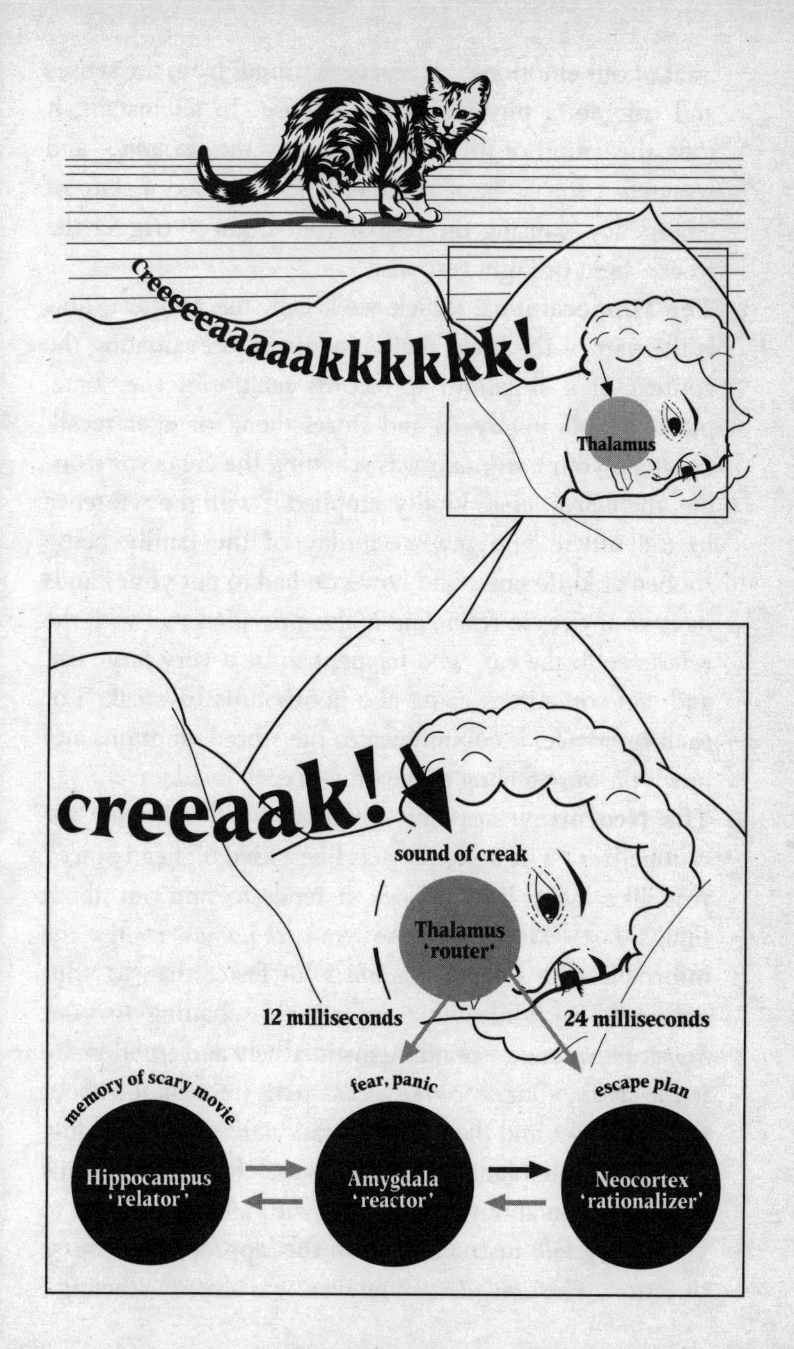
Creeeeeaaaaakkkkkk!
Thalamus
creeaak!
sound of creak
Thalamus
'router'
12 milliseconds
24 milliseconds
memory of scary movie
fear, panic
escape plan
Hippocampus
'relator'
Amygdala
'reactor'
Neocortex
'rationalizer'

'seat of our emotions'.[3] It reacts to stimuli from the senses and triggers a physiological response. In an instant, it took the sound of the creak routed by the *thalamus*, and scanned it for signs of trouble. Then it called a state of emergency, causing the rest of your brain to trigger the freeze, fight or flight response.

3. **The Hippocampus**: which we'll call 'the relator'. This is the part of the brain that is involved in evaluating the context of a situation. It records memories (i.e. time, place, people involved) and stores them for later recall. So when your *amygdala* was scanning the creak for trouble, the *hippocampus* kindly supplied it with the reference to the movie you saw yesterday of the family being robbed at knife point and how you had to put your hands over your eyes in fear. And it also provided you with the reference to the cat, who happens to be a very large cat, and can sometimes cause the floorboards to creak. For each reference, it communicates the stored emotions and how you were feeling at the time of each incident.
4. **The Neocortex**: last but not least, we'll call this 'the rationalizer'. The *neocortex* acts like a kind of 'head office'. And like many head offices, it tends to find out about things last. That's because your *thalamus* routes the information to your *amygdala* a lot faster than to your *neocortex*. So while your *amygdala* is chatting to your *hippocampus* and responding instinctively and emotionally to the creak, your *neocortex* picks up the information about the creak too, and then starts to rationalize it; organizing, analysing and planning. In this case, it sent a rational plan of action about how to deal with a burglar down to your *amygdala* instructing it on the 'appropriate' course of action. The *amygdala*, however, was already reacting.

This explains why, in the face of fear, our emotional response can override our rational thoughts. When the thalamus receives the sound of the creak, it routes it to the amygdala a lot quicker than to the neocortex (twelve milliseconds as opposed to the twenty-five milliseconds to the neocortex). That explains why we can 'act without thinking', especially in situations of intense pressure. What's also interesting is that the neuro pathway from the amygdala to the neocortex is stronger and more developed than the one going the other way. That's because our emotional systems have been around a lot longer than our rational mind. In fact, when we were born our neocortex was largely unformed, and the amygdala came with a genetically-implanted 'basic instinct' self. By the age of about two or three, enough experiences have taken place for the amygdala to develop and form emotional responses to specific events, people and places. These have formed the blueprint for all our instinctive reactions later in life. What's even more interesting is that at this age, because we don't have the neocortex development of language, logic and reasoning, our instinctual reactions to certain events may in fact seem quite irrational to our adult mind.

Gulp! Recap

When you feel fear:

- Your brain is wired to respond emotionally first and then rationally. The emotional centre of your brain gets this message before the rational centre, triggering an *instinctive fear response*.
- Something in the situation reminds you of an

emotionally charged prior experience, whether consciously or subconsciously.
- The fear trigger is likely to be sensory: a sound, tone of voice, image, taste, smell or touch.
- This causes a physiological body change that aims to help you freeze, fight or flee in order to survive a threat. Not the ideal place for making calm and rational choices!
- Even when your rational mind finally catches up and finds no real threat in the current situation, your emotional response may still override it due to the memory of past experiences.
- In fact, your *instinctive fear response* may appear irrational to you (and others), because it was hard-wired in the first two years of your childhood when you had very little reasoning ability.

Short Circuiting Fear

Gulp! Wisdom

Fear is only as deep as the mind allows.

Japanese proverb

Gulp! Time

Fear, then, is based on the brain's response to a perceived threat in the situation that you're facing. Your instinct is to respond emotionally, because your brain triggers an emotional response faster than a rational one. And the emotions you feel as a result trigger off an uncomfortable physiological response in your body like breathlessness, sweaty palms and a dry mouth, which can, in turn, actually feed your fear.

So if fear is triggered in your mind, then surely you can use your mind to manage it and reverse it. If you can master your mind, you'll be able to master your fear. And imagine what could be possible if you were less fearful about this Gulp! or any other one in the future.

The secret to short circuiting your fear is twofold:

1. Identifying what specifically is triggering your fear.
2. Finding ways to either eliminate the trigger or change what you feel about it.

Gulp! Wisdom

Between stimulus and response, there is a space.
In that space lies our freedom and power to
choose our response.
In our response lies our growth and freedom.
Viktor Frankl

Gulp! Time

Break It Down

When you break down fear into individual components, it's much easier to manage. That's because, rather than taking an 'all or nothing' approach where 'fear' becomes the big label for the whole situation, when you break it down into components you can start to see what specifically is causing the fear, and what is the source of the fear. It's a bit like saying 'my car's a wreck', when in actual fact most of your car is in tip top shape, it's just that your brake pads are a wreck.

Take Steve, for example. He's quite shy and is 'terrified of networking events', which is ironic given that he works in sales. For him, it's a real Gulp!. So he does everything he can to avoid going to events where networking plays a key role. When we dug underneath it, we discovered that in fact what he *enjoyed* about networking events was the free flowing fine wine and catching up with old colleagues. But this was always clouded by his fear of being stuck in a conversation with someone who kept droning on. It made him feel cornered, pinned down and unable to get away. So by identifying this specific trigger we were able to develop a simple strategy which allowed him to politely break off a conversation and move away. Now, armed with this new technique, Steve's much happier about going to networking events.

Once you've isolated the specific source of your fear, you can then focus on transforming this one component in the context of the bigger picture. Change this one thing, and you'll change the whole. That's because how you *feel* about the situation will influence how you act.

In the case of Steve, rationally speaking all he had to do was enter a large room where pleasant human beings, albeit a little tipsy, were clustered into small groups talking about the interesting developments at the exhibition. He simply needed to lift a glass of fine wine off the waiter's tray and go and join the small group of people in the middle of the room, open his mouth and contribute his opinion. If, rationally speaking, it was so simple, then why couldn't he do it? Why did he break out in a sweat just thinking about it? That's because of the emotionally charged feelings he had about the possibility of being stuck with someone who droned on. So before he'd even entered the room, he tensed up, became breathless and got sweaty palms (not ideal for handshaking which then triggered off another bout of fear of something else). Ironically, because of all of this, he often gravitated to the corner, and invariably *did* get cornered by someone.

So can you see how the *feeling* Steve had was completely based on *imagining* what might happen, which was heavily influenced by past scenarios. And that *feeling* created a physical sensation, just at the *thought* of it happening. But once we had developed a strategy that enabled him to politely escape a conversation, he *felt* more confident and quite relieved that he knew he could escape a situation that made him feel pinned down. So he could go into exactly the same networking event and have a completely different experience, simply because he had changed how he felt about it.

Same scenario. Different feeling. Different outcome.

It was no longer a Gulp!. So he no longer approached it from a place of fear. This is the power of feelings to dictate the action you take, or don't take, whatever the case may be.

How you *feel* about your Gulp! will prescribe how you react:

- A positive feeling will motivate a more optimistic proactive response.
- A negative feeling will motivate a fearful defensive response.
- A neutral feeling, on the other hand, will result in *procrastination*.

So if you suffer from procrastination and have ever wondered why, it's because the *feeling* isn't strong enough either way to tip you into action. Or a strong feeling is being counteracted by an equally negative feeling, completely neutralizing the overall feeling. Hence you sit on the fence and do nothing.

The trouble is that as you face your Gulp!, the feelings being induced are based on what you *imagine* might happen. They are based on a 'future possibility'. And it is your perception of this future possibility that determines how you're feeling and hence the action or inaction you take. Your perception is driven by what you know and what information you have. The simple fact is that once Steve was armed with new knowledge in the form of a technique, it completely changed the way he perceived exactly the same situation.

Gulp! Recap

As you face your Gulp!:

1. Your actions and how you respond will be based on your *feelings*.
2. How you feel about your Gulp! comes from *imagining* what might happen.
3. What you imagine comes from your *perception* of the situation.
4. And that all happens despite the *reality* of what is.

Gulp! Wisdom

Fear grows in darkness;
if you think there's a bogeyman around,
turn on the light.
Dorothy Thompson

Gulp! Time

The Challenge Cycle

As in the case of Steve, when we break down fear, we can identify the *fear trigger points* that are at the source of your fear. Change these, and you'll better master your fear. To help you do this, I've created The Challenge Cycle. This powerful cycle helps you to get a real handle on your current situation. It helps you to break down what is reality, and what is your perception. And it helps you identify how what you imagine might happen influences your feelings and therefore your reaction. Each stage represents a potential *fear trigger point*. Catch any one of them and change what you think and feel about it, and you'll change how you react and hence the outcome. Or putting it another way, change any one of them and you'll create a new reality.

The Challenge Cycle

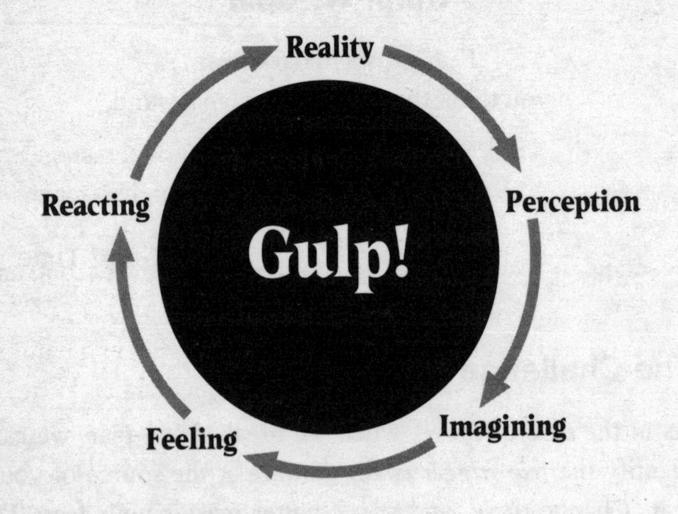

Reality	**What is the *reality* of your Gulp! situation?** Just like a detective at a crime scene, these are the cold facts about your situation including time, place, location, who is involved and any information about the scene that's important.
Perception	**What is your *perception* of your Gulp! situation?** This is where you look at your spin on the situation and consider the situation from your perspective. What do you believe is really going on, and how does this make you feel?
Imagining	**What do you *imagine* is happening or going to happen?** Now fast forward to the future and imagine

	what you think is likely to happen. What is the outcome likely to be?
Feeling	**How does this make you *feel*?** When you think of what might happen, this will naturally trigger an emotional response. How do you feel about what might happen?
Reacting	**And how do you naturally feel like *reacting* as a result?** Whatever you're feeling will trigger a natural reaction. You will feel compelled to take a particular course of action or behave in a certain way. When you think about the outcome you imagined, what action do you feel compelled to take?

Gulp! Wisdom

The voyage of discovery is not in seeking new landscapes but in having new eyes.

Marcel Proust

Gulp! Time

Let's look at Steve's networking event from two different perspectives.

Perspective One: 'Oh no, I'll get stuck with the gadget man'

Reality	**What is the *reality* of his Gulp! situation?** It is a networking event at an exhibition being held at the Excel Centre. It starts at 7pm and there will be approximately 200 people there from different companies. Fine wine and canapés will be served. It will end about 9pm.
Perception	**What is his *perception* of his Gulp! situation?** 'Oh gosh, not another networking event. While there are a few people I'd like to catch up with, it's going to be so crowded with loads of people I don't know, talking about inane things. And it clashes with the football match on TV.'
Imagining	**What does he *imagine* might happen?** 'I bet you I get there and while I am searching through the crowd for Tim and Sarah, I'll get cornered by that gadget supplier again who drones on and on. And I'll get stuck with him for the whole evening.'
Feeling	**How does this make him *feel*?** 'To be honest, I just can't bear the thought of getting stuck with that guy again. I dread it. And I don't feel at all enthusiastic about going. I really can't be bothered.'

Reacting **And how does he naturally feel like *reacting* as a result?**
'Well I guess I'll have to show my face because my boss will be there. So I'll pop in for ten minutes, walk around for a bit and then slip out and watch the football match in the bar.'

Perspective Two: 'Oh great, a chance to catch up with Tim and Sarah'

Reality **What is the *reality* of his Gulp! situation?**
It is a networking event at an exhibition being held at the Excel Centre. It starts at 7pm and there will be approximately 200 people there from different companies. Fine wine and canapés will be served. It will end about 9pm.

Perception **What is his *perception* of his Gulp! situation?**
'Oh great, a chance to catch up with Tim and Sarah and the crew. I haven't seen them for ages and it would be good to get the inside scoop on what's going on in their company. Wonder if there are any jobs going there? Shame about missing the football, though.'

Imagining **What does he *imagine* might happen?**
'Well, it should be a great evening. It might be hard to find Tim and Sarah in the crowd, so I'll probably text them when I get there. And if I see that gadget supplier heading towards me, I'll just use that technique

Gabriella showed me and then politely move on. I must remember to get my wife to tape the football though.'

Feeling	**How does this make him *feel*?** 'Actually, I'm looking forward to it. I've been run off my feet all week with this exhibition, talking shop, and it will be nice to relax a little and catch up with the crew. Who knows, I might even drum up some new business.'
Reacting	**And how does he naturally feel like *reacting* as a result?** 'Well I'll aim to get there by 7.30ish and then make a beeline for Tim and Sarah. I'm tired, so I probably won't last until the end but I'll stay a good hour.'

Same reality, same person, just a different perception. And therefore a different imagined outcome, different feelings and a different reaction.

It's clear, therefore, that fear and dread feed off your thoughts. Fearful feelings come from imagining fearful outcomes. And fearful feelings cause you to act fearfully.

Change how you feel about your Gulp! situation, and you'll completely change your attitude and your actions.

You can change all this simply by doing the following:

- **Know the Full Reality:**
  Find out more information about the situation. Look up facts and figures. Gather other people's opinions. Spend some time observing what is actually going on.

- **Change your Perception:**
  Be mindful of your thoughts. What are you thinking? What do you believe will happen? What is the negative voice saying? Think about the situation having a positive outcome.
- **Change your Imagining:**
  If you knew that the outcome could be positive, what are all the possibilities that could happen? Stretch your mind and imagine all the different options that could lead to a positive outcome.

Simply doing this exercise will raise your self-awareness, spark fresh insights and change your thinking. Once you bring these new insights into your conscious mind, then you'll add new information to your current perception, giving you a much fuller picture. In accordance with The Challenge Cycle, you are changing the baseline. So the fuller picture will lead to different imagined outcomes, different feelings which will in turn lead to different reactions.

It's as simple as that.

Gulp! Wisdom

Our world which we believe is so real,
is nothing more than the structures which we've created.

Dorothy Rowe

Gulp! Time

Gulp! Practice: The Challenge Cycle

Try the challenge cycle out for yourself. Note that this is an exploratory exercise at this point to help you get a better awareness and understanding of your perception, imagining and feeling about your current Gulp!

Take a fresh page in your journal and divide it into two columns as outlined below. Then complete the sentences:

Reality	**The best way to describe my current situation is that . . .**
	______________________________
	______________________________
	______________________________
Perception	**My perception of the current situation is . . .**
	______________________________
	______________________________
	______________________________
Imagining	**What I imagine might happen**
	a) if things worked out well is . . .
	______________________________
	______________________________
	______________________________
	b) if things worked out badly is . . .
	______________________________
	______________________________
	______________________________

Feeling **What I would feel**

a) if things worked out well is . . .

____

____

____

b) if things worked out badly is . . .

____

____

____

Reaction **So how I would tend to react**

a) if I focused on the positives is . . .

____

____

____

b) if I focused on the negatives is . . .

____

____

____

Write in your journal the three key insights you've gained from doing this exercise.

1. ________________________________
2. ________________________________
3. ________________________________

Ten Strategies to Master Fear

Gulp! Wisdom

Men are disturbed not by things,
but by the view which they take of them.
Epictetus

Gulp! Time

Based on everything we've talked about today, I hope that you are now fully aware that YOU create your own fear, and YOU have the power to disarm it. As you face your Gulp! use these ten simple strategies to help you master your fear when it crops up:

1. **Separate the reality from your perception.** We've seen that the reality of the situation is simply what is. And that it's your own unique perception that puts the spin on it and creates your fear. First of all, be rational and sort out the facts. Gather as much information as you can. Ask questions, investigate and do your research. Make sure you have the fullest picture possible of the true reality of your situation. Then do some soul searching, and explore your perceptions of the situation and why you're putting the 'spin' on it that you are.
2. **Identify the fear trigger points in the situation.** As you consider the current situation, rather than tar the whole situation with the 'I'm terrified of . . .' brush, isolate the specific aspects of the situation that trigger your fearful thoughts. By focusing on these you get to the nub of the

problem. Simply changing the way you look at these triggers or by creating strategies to deal with them, you'll immediately change the way you feel about your Gulp! and hence the way you react.

3. **Know where fear lives in your body.** Fear is an important indicator that tells you that something within you needs to be addressed. So the more in tune you are with your fear and where it lives in your body, the better you'll be able to deal with it in the moment. You'll also gain more awareness of your own physiological response to fear and where you carry the tension of your fear. If you are not aware of your fear, it will trigger your instinctive fear response, and you will be less in control of your actions. What you are aware of, you can deal with.
4. **Become an observer.** As soon as you become an observer of fear, then you're not 'in' it and reacting instinctively. When you are in observer mode, you are using your neocortex which, as we already know, is more rational and analytical, rather than being at the mercy of your impulsive amygdala. When you feel fear, simply observe what it is you are afraid of, and what specifically triggered it off. Then try and recall a past experience where something similar happened. Make the connection. Simply be aware of it, and collect this new information.
5. **Listen to your inner talk.** Did you notice that as you worked through this chapter there was quite a bit of chit chat going on in your mind? That's because when we talk about fear we are really shining the light on our inner beliefs and perceptions. The fear doesn't exist as such, you created it with your own thoughts. That's the benefit of facing your Gulp!. It brings your limiting thoughts to the surface so that you have to face them and address

them. When you do this you grow and develop as a person. So monitor the thoughts in your mind, and write them down in your journal. It can be a very insightful conversation!

6. **Create new associations.** The amygdala relies on the stories stored in the hippocampus as a guide on how to react. So you can manipulate this to create new associations for the same trigger. This is a very powerful concept. The classic case is imagining someone you fear in their swimsuit, or even naked. It lightens your whole outlook. Or remember Sue, who saw the big, strong, calm tree and fixed this in her mind to help her stay calm. So every time you think of your Gulp!, imagine a beautiful picture, or a piece of music or a person you love. If you do this regularly every day, very soon your brain, by its own natural instinct to store stories, will start to associate the Gulp! with something more pleasurable. Try it. It works.
7. **Consider the worst.** When you consider the worst that can happen, it can have a number of effects; you may sink into the depths of depression, or you may become even more committed to making sure that it doesn't happen. Let's face it, if you can imagine the worst in advance AND if you come up with plans and strategies to avoid that ever happening, then the likelihood of it happening will be small. So write down a scenario that leads to the worst outcome possible. Then look for the critical decisions or turning points on the way. What can you put in place to ensure that the worst case scenario never happens?
8. **Look at the glass half full.** We've seen the power of perception and how it influences the way you react and therefore the reality you create. If you think negatively,

it's likely you'll react defensively and create a less than satisfactory outcome. On the other hand, if you focus on the glass being half full, and look at all the positive aspects of your situation and all the things that could go right, you completely change your perception, and give yourself a much better chance of success. So imagine what a positive outcome would look like. Visualize this in your mind. Feel what it would be like. Practise this regularly and your thoughts will start to follow through and start to create a new reality.

9. **Learn how to create space.** Because the thalamus sends information to the emotional centre a lot faster than to the rational centre of the brain, when fear overwhelms you and your *instinctive fear response* does take over, learn to stop, create space and simply breathe. It is this instinctive reaction that is often detrimental. If you can learn to stop and create a moment of space, you open up the chance for you to react differently and for a different response to take place, because it gives time for your rational neocortex to catch up with your emotional amygdala. When you feel fear rising, simply stop, observe and breathe.
10. **Make it safe.** At the end of the day, when you feel safe, there is actually no need for the *instinctive fear response* to even kick in. So what do you need to do to create the safest environment possible? Like Sue, you can minimize the risk by carefully planning what you are going to do, and practising it again and again. Visit the place, go through the motions, do a dress rehearsal, create a routine for yourself. Top sports people do this all the time so that when they're under pressure they immediately slip into their routine and regain their focus.

Fear is a powerful teacher. At the end of the day it calls you to challenge the boundaries you've put around yourself. It calls you to challenge what you perceive, what you think and what you believe to be true. And it calls you to rise above it all and move to the next level of your potential.

Gulp! Day 2 Summary: Breakdown & Breakthrough

The five things to remember:

1. Fear starts in the brain. It is a physiological response to something you 'perceive' to be threatening. The same process that triggers fear can be used to reverse it.
2. Break down your fear and identify what is *the fear trigger point* and source of it all. Then, rather than tar the whole situation with the same brush, just work on the trigger points.
3. Change how you feel about your situation – what you feel determines how you act. Find a way to change your perception of the situation and look at the positives. This will trigger positive feelings which lead to positive actions.
4. Command your mind. The same inner voice that causes the negative chit chat so effectively can be used to shut it up or to communicate positive messages to your brain. So use a commanding voice. Strong, loud and clear.
5. Use the power of breath to slow down the impact of fear. Breathing not only calms the physiological symptoms of fear, it halts the *instinctive fear response*, creating space for something different to happen.

Gulp! Action Plan: Breakdown & Breakthrough

In facing my challenge, what I fear the most is:

____

____

____

____

My instinctive reaction is:

____

____

____

____

The fear trigger points are:

1. ______________________________________

2. ______________________________________

3. ______________________________________

Ways that I can eliminate or minimize these fear trigger points are:

1. ______________________________________

2. ______________________________________

3. ______________________________________

Ways that I can minimize the risk and maximize my sense of safety are:

1. ______________________________

2. ______________________________

3. ______________________________

I can create positive and uplifting associations with my challenge by:

____

____

____

____

____

Gulp! Espresso

Find a quiet space, grab a drink and spend a few moments just jotting down the first thoughts that pop into your head.

Gulp! Mediano

Find a quiet space and spend at least one hour really reflecting upon these questions. You might like to revisit them tomorrow.

Gulp! Grande

Over the coming week, spend some quiet time each day reflecting upon these questions. Set the intention to focus solely on your fears, breaking them down and understanding the triggers and beliefs underneath them. Really be honest with yourself. Take different perspectives. Peel back the layers and really see what's happening underneath.

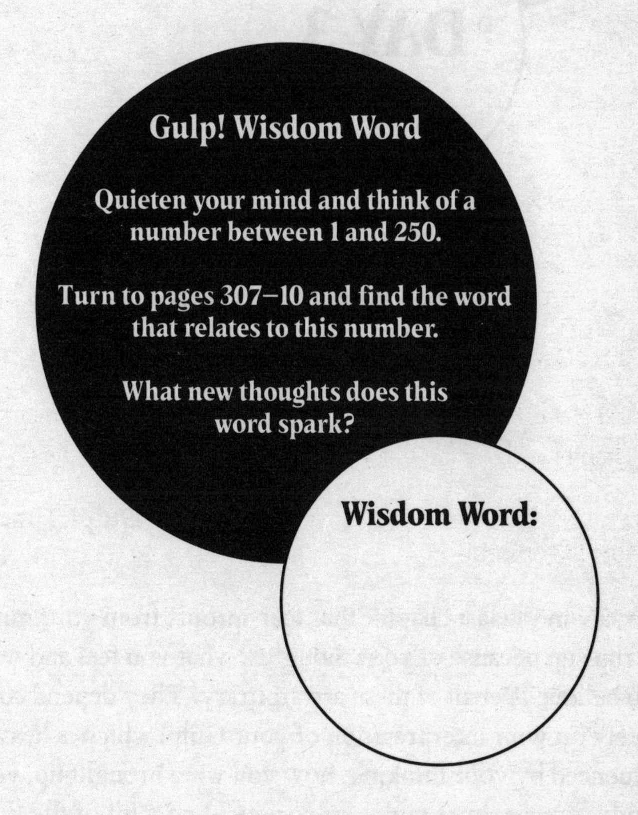

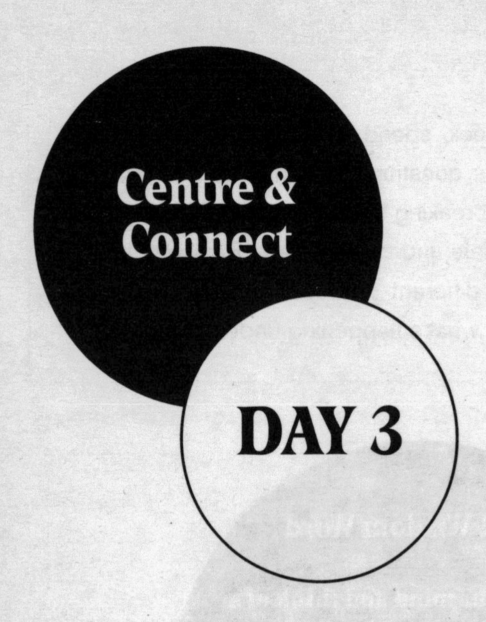

Gulp! Aims for Today

To silence the mind.
To access your deeper wisdom.
To feel more centred and connected.

Gulp! Time

We saw in the last chapter that fear sprouts from your mind. It crops up because of your thoughts, what you feel and what you believe. Yet all of these are arbitrary. They depend completely on your interpretation of your Gulp! which is heavily influenced by your thinking, how you were brought up, your family, your culture and your society. And a lot of the time, they're completely embedded in your subconscious. They guide you subliminally to make decisions and take actions. And they may no longer be appropriate for the situation you're facing right now.

So, what would happen if you could completely cut out the thoughts, feelings, beliefs, interpretations, judgements and assumptions?

It's simple. There is no fear. You're left with just 'what is'.

And so we come to the crux of the Gulp! philosophy. Just as martial artists stand calm and centred before they take swift and tactical action, so too can you approach your Gulp! in the same way. You can do this by completely cutting through the chit chat of your mind and reconnecting to your inner core. That place of inner calm. That place of purity. That place where everything is exactly as it's meant to be. That place where you can hear your inner wisdom, that deep knowingness that guides you to make the choices and actions that are true and right for you. I'm sure you've felt this deep knowing before, where you 'just knew' what you had to do. The best choices you make are the ones that come from this place. And the actions you take feel easy and graceful.

Imagine stepping up to your Gulp! and feeling calm, connected and certain? Today is about learning how.

Gulp! Wisdom

Connect to your core and you'll find strength.
Act from your core and you'll move mountains.

Gulp! Time

Returning to Your Core

The Chinese have a Taoist expression that describes returning to your core beautifully. *Wu-Ji*[1] (pronounced Wu Chi) *is the place of complete nothingness; the void that is beyond time and place, the point of origin for all that is*. Represented by an empty circle, this is where our mind, body and spirit are one, and unified. This is a place of complete stillness, a place of inaction and absolute quiet. This is the place of emptiness, of 'no thing'; no thoughts, no beliefs, no assumptions, no judgements. Just 'no thing'.

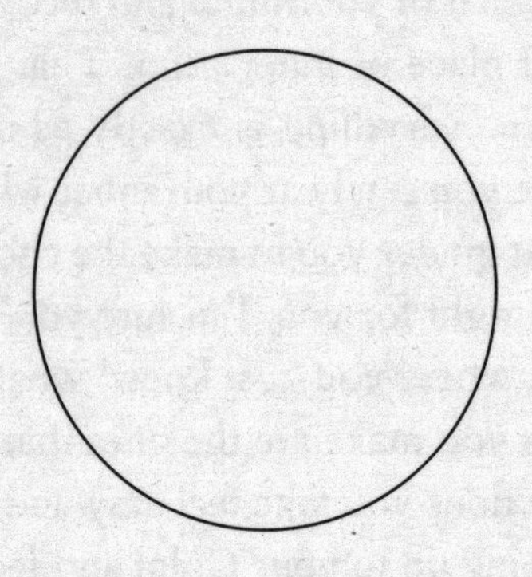

This is how we were born.
No thoughts. No beliefs. No judgements. No interpretations.
There is just what is.
Pure and simple.

Gulp! Wisdom

From 'no thing', movement arises naturally.
From inaction, comes action.
From emptiness, come shape and form.
And from stillness, come energy and flow.

Gulp! Time

Cutting Through the Chit Chat

But the reality is that our inner core has been layered by the interpretations of our thoughts, beliefs, feelings, attitudes, behaviours and judgements. These have been shaped by our upbringing, our culture and our society. From a very young age we learn what's 'right' and what's 'wrong'. When we look at our Gulp!, we get stuck in the 'story', or rather our interpretation of the story of what's going on. We get caught up in the trials and tribulations happening on the surface, as our ego mind tries to manage our way out of the situation and control the outcome. The worry, anxiety and nervousness that this creates is incredibly draining, leaving us in a weakened physical, mental and emotional state to actually step up to the Gulp!

But are you seeing the situation for what it truly is? Can you really see all the possibilities and outcomes available to you? Or is your sight being clouded by the seductive nature of your thoughts and beliefs that only see your situation from one perspective? And are these thoughts truly your own, or how much are they actually being influenced by those of your family and culture?

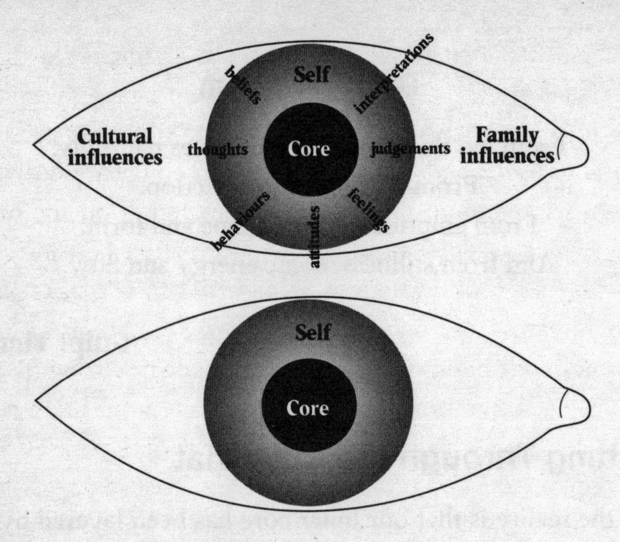

The way to cut through the clutter and connect with our true nature, the essence of who we are underneath all the conditionings of society, our culture and family, is to silence the mind and empty it of thoughts. Sounds rather dramatic, I know, but when we can sink below what is happening on the surface and connect to the deeper meaning for the Gulp! we face, we start to see what is real, rather than what is made up by our thoughts and interpretations. And then what we create from this place is pure and true. It is unified and aligned to the core of our true being. And when we act from this place, our actions become strong, powerful and imbued with pure intentions.

Silencing Your Thoughts

The problem with today's twenty-first century living, though, is that we rarely take the time to silence our thoughts and empty our minds. Instead, we constantly fill them with chit chat, recycling the same thoughts and interpretations that go on to fuel our worries, fears and anxieties. Sometimes it gets so bad that we literally can't hear ourselves think.

When you silence your mind you create a gap in your chit chat. And it is in this gap that you create space for mysterious things to happen. That's because our chit chat goes on in our conscious mind. Our subconscious mind, on the other hand, which is rich with helpful information and insights, hardly gets a look in, except at night when it speaks to us in our dreams. Our subconscious mind accounts for ninety per cent of our brain power. And we're just not using it.

By silencing your mind and returning to your inner core, you're doing two things. First, you are providing yourself with a valuable contrast so that you become more aware of how much chit chat really goes on in that mind of yours. Secondly, you're providing the space and time for new information and new ideas to pop through from your subconscious.

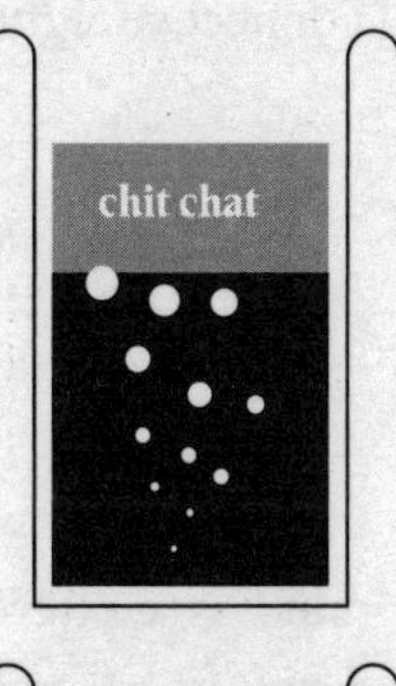

Inner wisdom, fresh insights and fizzing ideas bubbling up, but can't get through the chit chat.

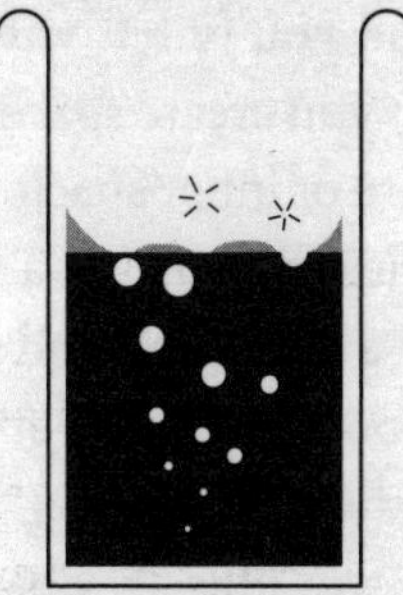

When you silence the mind and shut up the chit chat, you create space for the inner wisdom, fresh insights and fizzing ideas to pop to the surface.

These fresh insights and nuggets of inner wisdom may be enough to completely transform the way you approach your Gulp!. It's a bit like having a super fast broadband connection to your own inner google search engine, rather than the normal dial-up modem access that most of us have today. You'll be able to peel back the layers of your assumptions and judgements, and see your situation from a truer perspective. What's more, because the contrast between 'chit chat' and 'no thing' is so dramatic, you'll start to realize how much chit chat actually goes on, and how much it rules your life.

Gulp! Wisdom

Listen to your mind, and you'll tire
quickly of its discourse.
Silence your mind, and you'll connect straight
back to source.

Gulp! Time

Creating Space to Be

It is incredible how much of our mind is cluttered with thoughts. When you silence the mind you're left with some breathing space to simply 'be'. When you create space, you'll notice a sense of expansion and a sense of inner spaciousness. You'll feel the weight of your worries lift off. It's a bit like taking off a pair of tight jeans after a big meal, and feeling everything expand again. What's more, when you still your mind you slow down your brain waves, allowing you to access greater creativity and intuition. This is what I call 'smart thinking'. In the same way that you 'sleep on a problem' and invariably wake up with the solution because it's popped through from your subconscious mind, so too can you contemplate your Gulp! during your periods of reflection time. Often the answer will 'pop' through into your conscious mind, saving you hours of worrying and fretting. This really is smart thinking. That's because when you calm the mind you slow down your brain waves, from the faster *beta wave* state, to the slower *alpha wave* and *theta wave* states, giving you access to deeper levels of your own insight, wisdom, intuition and creativity. Stuff that's already there, but you're so busy in the frantic *beta wave* states of chit chat and do do, that you can't access the rich resource that lies within you already.

Beta State: (waves range between 14 and 40 Hz). Here you are wide awake and alert. Your mind is sharp and focused. Your cognition and concentration are high.
Alpha State: (waves range between 8 and 13 Hz). Here you are deeply relaxed, but not in a meditative state. You're able to access deeper levels of creativity and to practise visualization.
Theta State: (waves range between 4 and 7 Hz). Here you are in a deep meditative state, but not quite asleep. Known as the twilight zone, it brings about a dreamlike state that enables you to access your deep intuition and long-term memory.
Delta State: (waves range between 0 and 3Hz). Here you are in a deep sleep, where the body is healing itself and accessing your deep subconscious (that's why 'sleeping on a problem' often yields good results).[2]

I want to encourage you to start creating space in your life TODAY, to give you the chance to connect to your core and centre yourself *before* you make any decisions or take any action. You'll find that if you take time out to silence your mind, connect to your core and create that inner space for new insights and creativity to emerge, just like the martial artists, you'll end up only taking the action that 'feels right' for you. Hence you save a lot of needless worrying, you're confident about your decisions, you remain balanced and you get in the flow.

Gulp! Wisdom

Create space simply to 'be'
and clarity emerges for you to see.

Gulp! Time

A colleague of mine, Aboodi, shared a wonderful story with me about his experience of centring himself. He'd started a reflection practice as a result of doing a Leadership Training Course. Despite himself(!), he'd kept this practice going daily. One of the most interesting and rewarding benefits he found was the way it's enabled him to get back to his centre more quickly than before. 'Centre, like balance, is for me, not a place to live, but a place to visit,' says Aboodi. 'Life comes along and throws us off centre all the time. The trick is to catch ourselves being thrown off centre, and then to bring ourselves back to centre, as soon as we can, rather than to avoid being thrown off centre in the first place.' His daily practice soon paid off. One afternoon he was driving to meet a friend, tired from not having slept well. He was also running late, and then got lost. He immediately started to overreact, getting angry and flustered. He became aware of what he was doing, and pulled over to the side of the road, reconnected with his centre, and then asked someone for directions. He continued on his journey, very different from his pre-practice days when he would have stayed frustrated, and carried on driving, winding himself up more and more. 'Now, here's the thing – the only reason the option of noticing that I was off centre and doing something about it was available to me was because I had been practising regularly,' finishes Aboodi.

This is the beauty of having a regular practice of stillness, silence and reflection. Not only does it help you find your centre, it provides you with a new benchmark to help you realize when you're off centre.

Kate's experience is similar. She regularly practises breathing and meditation exercises she learnt at the local Buddhist Centre. 'A lot of the time, I'm trying to concentrate but the truth is that my mind is going off shopping,' laughs Kate. But through regular practice she has noticed that she is more accepting of situations and doesn't get as angry or irritated as she used to when things don't go her way. 'I've realized that if you've got a calm and peaceful mind, it doesn't matter what's going on outside of you because it just doesn't trouble you.'

Five Powerful Ways to Centre and Connect

The techniques we're covering today are aimed at helping you silence your mind and find inner calm. They act as portals to accessing your inner wisdom. When you practise the techniques, you'll also start to notice yourself feeling more centred and surefooted. That's because you *are* more centred in who you are, and aligned to your core. This will help you enormously to deal with anything, or anyone, that might attempt to throw you off course as you step up to your Gulp!.

I recommend that you read through them all, try them out and then pick the ones that resonate most strongly with you. Some will work for you better than others. I've also included the insightful wisdom from experts who regularly practise these techniques and who have dedicated their lives to helping people connect to their core and true nature.

I practise all of the techniques myself on a regular basis, and they have completely transformed my ability to respond to challenging situations. Now, whenever I face a Gulp!, the first thing I do is centre myself, silence my thoughts and use my inner wisdom to reflect upon the situation and solutions. I create space for the answers to emerge. The results are incredible. I have become more certain, more confident and more centred in myself. And I know I can access this anytime, anyplace and anyhow.

None of these strategies are complicated; in fact they will remind you to get back to basics, to things you already know deep down inside. The beauty is actually in their simplicity.

1. Cultivating Stillness and Silence
2. Presencing Yourself
3. Breathing for Life
4. Synchronizing with Music
5. Connecting with Nature

Strategy 1: Cultivating Stillness and Silence

Gulp! Wisdom

The stillness envelops me leaving nowhere to hide.
It shows me that which I know I must see,
but fear deep inside.
For my life is exactly what I have created it to be,
And face this challenge is what I must do,
in order to be free.

Gulp! Time

Have you ever experienced a stillness so silent that you could almost hear it? In truth, in today's city lifestyle it is very rare to experience such profound stillness on a regular basis, unless you wake up at dawn when everyone else is asleep. So I envy those of you who live in the countryside, miles away from busy streets and honking cars.

When you find that place of inner stillness, something magical happens. In this place you can actually hear your true self. The world suddenly seems simpler, your worries and anxieties fall away and you find a place of deep inner peace where it feels like everything is exactly as it's meant to be. Even in a place of real challenge, this inner reassurance can make complete and utter sense. It makes you realize how much time you actually spend *off centre*.

The voice that you hear in this place is from your wiser self, the one that truly knows what is best for you. It's not the mind that is egocentric, looking at how you can control and manage the situation around you, but the wise inner voice that truly knows what is best for you and your life in its most authentic sense.

Every year I am invited to speak at a retreat for people who work in the prison service, which is held by the Brahma Kumaris at their retreat centre on the outskirts of Oxford. The Brahma Kumaris are a spiritual organization founded in India in the 1930s and dedicated to meditation, self-transformation and spreading peace around the world. From humble roots, they have expanded in leaps and bounds over the past seventy years with over 4,500 centres in sixty-six countries. Rather uniquely for today's spiritual organizations, they are led by women, who are responsible for managing the centres and doing the spiritual teaching. Men play a supporting role in administration and the more heavy duty work like gardening and driving. Their retreat centre at Nuneham Park, just outside of Oxford, is a beautiful place and I carry very fond memories of the picturesque gardens and tranquil setting, ideal for chilling out and reflecting upon life. As I travel up to Oxford on the train, I'm always conscious of the tension and knots in my shoulders and the furrow in my brow. But as soon as we near Oxford, I immediately feel myself relaxing, almost muscle by muscle, at the thought of what awaits me. And when the taxi driver drops me off at the entrance of this amazing English manor house and I step into the reception area, I am met with a profound stillness so strong, it's almost tangible. It is so still you can almost hear the silence. Instantly, my breathing slows down, my body slows down and I feel a profound sense of inner calm. It is like entering a world where there is no time. My thoughts slow down, my worries slow down and my mouth relaxes into a soft smile. Within hours I feel balanced and centred within myself. Any Gulp! I'm facing suddenly feels more achievable, and the way forward becomes clear. It's a bit like the archaeologist who dusts away the soil to reveal the golden coin hidden within. It was always there, it was just shrouded by the soil.

This is the power of stillness.

'*There is a part of you that is perfect and pure*,' says Dadi Janki in her book *Companion of God*.[3] '*It is untouched by the less than perfect characteristics you've acquired by living in a less than perfect world. This part of you is a Still-Point – a deep, enriching experience of Silence*.' Dadi Janki heads the Brahma Kumaris in Europe and I think she is one of the greatest spiritual leaders of modern times. Standing at under five feet tall, she has a formidable presence, and is equally comfortable meeting the dignitaries at the United Nations as she is the probation officers that work in the UK's toughest prisons. Her story is an inspirational one, as captured by Liz Hodgkinson in *The Story of the Brahma Kumaris*,[4] and I'd like to share some of it with you.

Born in Sind in 1916 at a time when women were without education and rights, Dadi Janki knew from an early age that marriage and a family were not for her. Unfortunately, her father didn't agree and married her off at the age of twenty. She'd already attended some gatherings held by Brahma Baba, the founder of the Brahma Kumaris, and had that strong feeling that she'd found her true calling. But her husband had different ideas. He wanted her as his wife and literally kept her prisoner at home for fourteen months, trying to force her to conform, often resorting to violent and brutal measures. But Dadi Janki found ways to assert her independence. In one of her interviews with Liz Hodgkinson she recalls, '*Through these challenges, my internal strength grew*.' One day she developed enough inner strength and escaped, fleeing to Karachi to finally join the Brahma Kumaris. Since then she has truly lived her calling, spear-heading the international expansion of the Brahma Kumaris and helping to establish meditation and spiritual centres in over sixty-six countries. She gained further prominence when the Brahma Kumaris were given affiliation at the United Nations as a Non-Governmental Organization, and in 1986 she launched the Million Minutes of Peace Appeal, one of the largest non-fundraising projects for the UN. In early 1990 she was formally recognized as one of the Keepers of Wisdom, a group of distinguished spiritual leaders who came together at a large UN meeting to bring a spiritual perspective to global critical issues.

You'd think that at ninety years of age she would slow down. But oh no, not Dadi Janki. Just listening to her 'schedule of service' can make you feel exhausted. Her stam-ina is legendary, and she shows little sign of slowing down. I was fascinated to learn more about how she finds such inner strength and clarity of thought in the midst of such a busy schedule and daily challenges. Few people can keep up with her. Fortunately, I caught her between trips and was granted an interview. She'd just arrived from the Philippines and was leaving again in a week to go to India and then Sao Paulo. It was a great honour to be joined by Sister Jayanti, who co-founded the Brahma Kumaris in England with Dadi Janki in 1974, and who translated for us.

When you meet Dadi Janki, you're always struck by her childlike nature. She literally springs barefoot into the room, encased in a white sari, with a cheeky smile on her face and a twinkle in her eye. You immediately know that you're in the presence of greatness, yet you don't feel intimidated. In fact, it's a very humbling experience. There is a complete absence of ego, and you are left with the purity that is Dadi Janki.

It is through a regular practice of silence and stillness that Dadi Janki has been able to achieve the phenomenal feats that she has. She shares with me her thoughts on how she manages it.

Silence, Stillness and Reflection Time underpin the Brahma Kumari ethos, and that's why their centres are such havens of peace and quiet. Dadi Janki, herself, wakes every morning at four am and starts the day with early morning meditation for at least an hour. She does this every day. It is through silence and her connection to God that she accumulates her inner power, mental clarity and courage. And her energy and drive are legendary.

Have High Quality Thoughts. As we've already seen, your thoughts are at the source of all your actions. 'When your mind is pure and clean, your life will reflect this as well,' says Dadi Janki. 'God wants us to be instruments to spread love, peace and happiness.' So she focuses on having high quality thoughts. This, she says, keeps her light.

Free Yourself From Desire. 'I am the master of my own mind,' Dadi Janki states emphatically. 'So I free my mind from desires and attachments. When I free myself from all desires I stay light. When I am light everything works out well.' This is really insightful. If you think of attachments metaphorically they *do* tie you down, so it's easy to become heavy and stuck. But when you free yourself from being attached to things you are no longer tied, and you do become lighter and able to move freely.

Be Present. When I spoke with Dadi Janki her attention was completely focused on me the whole time. 'Wherever I'm present, I am fully present; happy and powerful,' says Dadi Janki. 'My time is well used and so is yours. Every thought is powerful and every moment is useful.' She says that many people waste time worrying and thinking about things that are not useful. Will have to raise my hand to that one!

Inner Preparation. Obstacles come and go. Sometimes they can cause great upheaval, and other times they keep reappearing. 'When you are afraid, then the obstacle becomes more powerful,' says Dadi Janki. 'I make sure I keep my consciousness free from obstacles. And through silence, I do the inner preparation that helps me deal with them if they come my way. Then, the obstacle comes, but it doesn't shake my stage.'

She finishes off by chuckling, 'I don't consider myself to be an old lady. And I don't allow my intellect to be dull or weak because of age. Why be ordinary and mediocre? Do something new every day.'

Wise words indeed, from an extraordinary woman.

Gulp! Practice: Cultivating Stillness and Silence

What happens when you sit in silence? Make a point to experience stillness today:

1. Find a quiet place and just sit in silence for five to fifteen minutes.
2. Notice what happens when you sit in silence.

3. Observe what goes on in your mind and body.
4. Ask yourself, 'What can't I be with?'

Strategy 2: Presencing Yourself

Gulp! Wisdom

In the present, there is only the here and now.
For the past is gone, and the future has yet to arrive.

Gulp! Time

Life happens in the present. And each thought, feeling and action made in the present creates the platform for what happens in the next moment. Our current thoughts create our future reality. When you are mindful of what is going on in the present, you're more likely to have a truer and more real perspective. You're more likely to see the serendipitous clues that cross your path. And you're more likely to make better decisions because you are basing them on what is happening now, rather than on what happened in the past (which is gone) and what has yet to happen (which might not even come to pass).

When I lived in Mexico, I had a very patient meditation teacher called Miguel. He gave us a phrase to repeat to ourselves in the attempt to stay focused, '*No hay pasado, no hay futuro, solo hay presente*' (There is no past, there is no future, there is only the present). At first I was perplexed. Of course there was a past, and of course there is a future I'm moving towards. So how can it not be? After a great deal of contemplation, the penny finally started to drop.

At any moment in time *there is only the present*. The past is over and the future has yet to be created by us. So there is only the present moment, like NOW (click your fingers), and NOW, and NOW. In each of these moments we have a choice about what we want to create in that moment. What we want to think in that moment. What we want to do in that moment. And how we want to react in that moment. The result of which leads to the creation of the next moment.

While I meditated on this, I realized that I did spend rather a lot of my time living in the future; imagining, planning and doing quite a bit of worrying. Others in the group spent a lot of time living in the past; reminiscing, analysing and regretting. Very few of us were actually mindful of being in the present moment. This was, in fact, a very novel thought in itself.

Experience presencing yourself for a moment. Put the book down and become truly present to your surroundings. Really look at the things around you. Notice their colour, their texture and what feelings they evoke in you. Listen for sounds all around you, even behind you. Empty your mind of all thoughts. Simply focus on the objects or people around you, casually observing and noticing what you see with a detached view. Check in with your body and notice how you are feeling. Observe your posture and any tension that you hold in your body. Relax. Observe. Just notice.

You are now fully present. Quite simple really, isn't it?

This is the place that brings wonderful opportunities for creating what has yet to be created. This is the place where quantum shifts can be made. And this is the place where you can influence what is happening right here and now because you are focused on your 'current reality', rather than your 'possible future' or 'perceived past'.

So why is it so difficult to do?

Eckhart Tolle has written an enlightening book called *The Power of Now*.[5] To be honest, I found it pretty heavy going the first time around because my mind is so often in the future and bringing it back to the present took quite a bit of patience and perseverance to say the least. In his book, Tolle talks about how we have become compulsive thinkers, and being unable to stop thinking has become an affliction that most people suffer from. This incessant mental noise makes up interpretations of what is going on around us causing stress and, in the process, prevents us from finding that realm of inner stillness that comes from being in the present moment. And you can't find the present moment as long as you're in your mind! He explains that when your thoughts subside, it creates a gap of 'no-mind'. At first the gaps will be short, a few seconds perhaps, but gradually they will become longer. It's when these gaps occur that you feel a certain stillness and peace inside you.

It goes without saying that when you are in this state, you're more awake and alert. You're centred in the here and now, rather than being pulled into the 'what might have been' or 'what might be'. Most of all, as you learnt in the last chapter, when you are in this place you are devoid of the thoughts which trigger your feelings of fear, impatience and frustration which put you off balance and drain your energy. You are left with purity, peace and quiet.

Gulp! Practice: Presencing Yourself

As you prepare yourself to step up and Gulp!, listen to your mind chatter. Where are your thoughts? Are they on the unknown future, working out or worrying about every possible scenario? Or are they on the past, lamenting what could have been?

Quieten your mind and bring yourself into the present:

1. Be conscious of your thoughts. From now on, be conscious of where your thoughts are. Being conscious of your mind's chit chat is the first step to managing it.
2. Practise being in the present. Take every opportunity that you can to bring yourself into the present. You could be sitting on the bus, or walking to work, or chilling out at home. Simply stop your thoughts and focus on being in the here and now.
3. Use all your senses. Listen to the sounds, notice the smells, feel the chair beneath you and the ground beneath your feet, see the vibrancy of colours, feel the textures of objects and sense the mood around you.
4. Stay detached. Don't attach any particular meaning or interpretation on what you notice as you presence yourself. Simply relax, observe and just notice.
5. Be patient. Once you start presencing yourself you'll realize how much mind chit chat really goes on in that head of yours. And what's worse, something that seems so simple like not thinking can be incredibly difficult to achieve and sustain. Be patient with yourself, and practise at every opportunity.

Strategy 3: Breathing for Life

Gulp! Wisdom

Breathing is the essence of life.
Breathe deeply, live fully.

Gulp! Time

Breathing is such an intrinsic part of our life that we don't even notice we're doing it until we walk into a hot stuffy room, run up the stairs or have a panic attack and suddenly find it difficult to breathe. Breathing is essential to life. We breathe in oxygen from the air around us and this gets absorbed into the bloodstream by the lungs.[6] The heart then pumps the oxygenated blood to all of the body's seven trillion cells which use the oxygen to produce energy. In turn, the cells release waste products including carbon dioxide and water which are then absorbed and carried away by the blood to be expelled.

Oxygen, therefore, is the cornerstone of breathing and for life. So what has breathing got to do with your big Gulp!?

First of all, breathing is a great way of calming yourself when you feel the pressure, because it brings more oxygen into your body. Secondly, because breathing is the very essence of life, focusing on your breath is a powerful way for you to connect to your inner core.

Breathing to Calm Yourself

When you are facing a Gulp! that causes you stress, whether real or imagined, as we've seen already your body responds instinctively causing hyperventilation and quick, shallow breathing. Dennis Lewis, a long-time student of Taoism and teacher of authentic breathing, qigong, and meditation, is the author of *Free Your Breath, Free Your Life*.[7] In doing the research for my book, I had a wonderful conversation with Dennis. He explained to me that this type of stressed breathing will sharply reduce the level of carbon dioxide in your blood. And this causes the arteries, including the carotid artery going to the brain, to constrict, reducing the flow of blood throughout the body. When this happens, no matter how much oxygen you may breathe into your lungs, your brain and body will experience a shortage of oxygen because they depend on the blood flow. This lack of oxygen triggers the sympathetic nervous system – your 'fight or flight reflex' – which makes you tense, anxious and irritable. As a result, it inhibits your ability to think clearly, and puts you at the mercy of your fearful thoughts.

'If you see you're in a stressed-out state then the first thing is to come into your body, feel your feet on the floor, feel the earth supporting you, sense your feelings in the body,' explains Dennis from his home in San Francisco. 'The minute you notice your breathing you'll begin to notice whether it's constricted, or fast. Don't react to it, or try to change it right away. Simply allow yourself to be with it and observe.' This in itself can be calming. By focusing on the breath, your thoughts immediately move away from the anxieties of the mind and calm it. As we become more conscious of our breathing, we are then able to bring it back to a natural balance. We become calmer.

When you practise this simple approach on a regular basis, you train your mind to respond to stress in a different way. That's because you are taking control of your own instinctive fear responses. And the simple act of breathing will bring more oxygen into your body and brain.

You'll start to notice that:

- you are able to remain relatively calm even in high stress situations.
- you are able to bounce back quickly if you're thrown off course.
- your muscles are more relaxed and your bodily functions work more effectively.
- your mind becomes calmer and you can easily focus your attention.
- your thinking becomes clearer and you open yourself to higher creativity.

What's more, while the situation you are in might still wind you up, you become less affected by it because you are calm and not responding reactively in the first place.

Breathing to Connect to Your Core

'To be centred means to be in touch with our body, mind and emotions, and have these different parts integrated,' says Dennis Lewis. 'Our mind drives most things; fear, anxiety and all the stories we surround ourselves with. Whatever's happening in the mind is always reflected in our breathing.

So when our breathing is narrow, restricted and tight we can be sure that there's something going on emotionally. And you can be sure that there is some guiding thought, agenda or habitual thought structure or judgement underneath it.'

Breathing can keep you grounded. That's because breathing always happens in the present moment. When you become conscious of your natural breathing, your attention immediately moves from your thoughts in the mind, to the breath in your body and therefore into the present moment. Your conscious awareness starts to expand, and with this comes a sense of inner spaciousness. And as your inner space expands, your thoughts appear to diminish by comparison. This connects you back to the wholeness of your inner core.

Dennis is a huge advocate of 'natural breathing', that is, not trying to manipulate it through complicated breathing techniques, rather simply being mindful of your breathing and adjusting your posture to free it up where it might be blocked. It is through this detached observation that we start to be more aware of what is happening with the breath and why we are breathing that way. This awareness of our breath brings greater clarity.

And while your thoughts and emotions might periodically cloud your vision of what's really happening as you step up to Gulp!, they don't shift you off centre because of your strong connection to your inner core.

Gulp! Practice: Breathing for Life

Start the practice of conscious natural breathing today and practise it daily.

It's really simple. Before getting out of bed in the morning become aware of your breathing:

- Is it deep or shallow?
- Is it fast or slow?
- Is it flowing or strained?
- Is your out-breath longer than your in-breath?
- Where does your breath seem to be getting stuck?

Continue this for between five and ten minutes or longer if you wish. For added effect:

- Practise presencing yourself and silencing your mind.
- Adjust your posture or body to free your breath.

To further enhance the impact of natural breathing awareness, and to really clear your head and focus your mind, conduct this practice in a still place; outside in a park, near some trees, by the seaside or even on the top of a hill or mountain.

Note: If you get breathless or dizzy at any point, simply stop the practice and just breathe normally.

Strategy 4: Synchronizing with Music

Gulp! Wisdom

Music when it hits that special note
Unleashes my spirit and sends it soaring,
Taking it to a place where angels roam
Connecting me to my true calling.

Gulp! Time

Another powerful way of calming the mind and allowing you to reconnect to your inner core is through music, sound and harmonics. They are powerful forces in our life and can make our heart sing and our feet dance. They can lift our spirits and soothe our soul. They can cut across generations, races and nations, expressing the feelings that words cannot speak. And they can pull the heart strings of even the most hardened person. Music is a powerful form of self-expression, one that unites people, and has been an integral part of our lives since the beginning of time.

I'm reminded of a time many years ago when I went to Cardiff to watch the All Blacks, New Zealand's rugby team, play Wales. As is the custom at the start of the game, the Welsh fans stood up to sing their national anthem. They stood together in their red shirts, scarves and woolly hats creating a sea of red. Then they started to sing. Nothing can prepare you for the power and impact of over 50,000 fiercely patriotic Welsh men and women singing the national anthem in unison. Even to this day I can remember that special moment when all those wonderful voices synchronized and united, producing a single harmonized tone that reverberated throughout the stadium. It made the hairs stand up on the back of my neck. When it was New Zealand's turn to sing, we truly did our best. Greatly outnumbered we tried to make up for it by singing louder, or rather shrieking louder. The truth is that we sounded like strangled cats. Our only consolation was that we went on to win the game.

So what has music got to do with stepping up to your Gulp!?

Music, sounds and singing have the power to change our physiology; our breathing, the beat of our heart, our muscle tension and our endorphins. It can slow us down, speed us up and even clear the head. Don Campbell has written extensively on the impact that music, sound and vibration have on health, learning and behaviour, and is the author of *The Harmony of Health* and *The Mozart Effect*.[8] In these fascinating books, he cites the research of Dr Tomatis, the renowned Frenchman who has dedicated his life to a new multi-disciplinary science called Audio-Psycho-Phonology (APP), which shows that the rhythms, melodies and high frequencies of Mozart's music stimulate and charge the creative regions of the brain. Dubbed the 'Mozart Effect', it is proven to calm the listener, improve spatial perception and help people express themselves more clearly. Large chunks of this book have been written with Mozart playing in the background.

This is the power of music and sound.

What I find most intriguing is the impact that pulse, pace and pattern or structure can have on setting your mood, and how you can literally organize the pace and rhythm of your day by how you organize the music you play. We've all seen great athletes deep in focus listening to their MP3 players before a race to help them get into 'the zone'. According to Don Campbell in *The Mozart Effect*, that's because our bodies like natural order, and will physically adjust to the pace, pulse and rhythm of the music we are listening to. The blend of the beat, the melody and the tone can bring a kind of synchronized order to our bodies, just as a fine sand forms intricate patterns when it's placed on top of a vibrating drum or a speaker.

Music can integrate the mind and body, stimulating or calming the brain in the process. And this effect is not limited to humans. When I was a child, I remember staying on a farm and getting up early to milk the cows. The farmer, a rugged man in his black singlet and muddy gumboots, looked quite out of sync with the melodious classical music coming out of the rather battered radio hanging precariously from a post.

As you face your Gulp!, let music and sound be a powerful ally. First, you can use it to calm your mind, and secondly, you can use it to help you clarify your thinking. Thirdly, you can use it to help you manage your emotions and fourthly, you can use it to find your true voice.

Calming Your Mind

According to Don Campbell, music with a pulse of approximately sixty beats a minute can shift our brain waves from the *beta wave* state (alert and concentrated), to the slower waves of the *alpha wave* state (relaxed). The heart normally beats at between sixty-five and seventy-five beats per minute, so the slower beat of this music helps to slow down the heart if it's racing from stress or fear. In addition, slow music has more space within the tones and creates a sense of mental 'space', allowing your mind to relax and float freely. Listening to slower Baroque music (Bach, Handel, Vivaldi), New Age music, Gregorian chants and ambient music, are excellent for calming your mind. Try some Shamanic drumming, and you can go even deeper into the *theta wave* state (dreamlike state).

Clarifying Your Thinking

Mozart's music with its melodic clarity and elegance is apparently very good for clearing the mind, organizing the thoughts and making sense of things. That's because not only does it have a slower pace, but the notes are well ordered and structured, and blended melodies are uncomplicated. For me, there is something about James Blunt's album *Back to Bedlam*; the slow pace and pure simplicity of his music really helped me to get into 'the zone' to write. Whenever I lost my train of thought, simply listening to a few songs helped my muddled thoughts somehow settle into a simple order.

Managing Your Emotions

Anger, angst, sorrow, joy, courage, passion and even hate are all emotions that find their expression through music. From Eminem's anthems of anger, to Destiny's Child's rendition of 'I'm a Survivor', whatever the emotion, you'll find music that expresses it. In some cases, this is because the musician or singer expresses personal emotion through the words of the song and what they bring to the performance. Other times it's because a piece of music or a song holds a powerful memory for us; first love, heartbreak or fun summer holidays.

In this way, music can be a powerful mood shifter or mood builder. As you face your Gulp! you can help manage your mood by selecting music to play when you want to reflect, or to feel inspired, or to find courage or to vent your anger.

Spend a few moments now to consider the following emotions. What music or song springs to mind that inspires this emotion in you?

disappointment ______________________

courage ______________________

passion ______________________

love ______________________

laughter ______________________

Finding Your True Voice

Our own voices also provide a powerful means of reconnecting to our core. Stewart Pearce, in his book *The Alchemy of Voice*,[9] speaks about each one of us having our own unique 'signature note'. '*We are all unique, and particularly we each have our own note, our own vibration. This is the "signature sound" of our being: individual, distinctive and unlike that of any other person.*' (Page 52.)

I went to see Stewart to find out more and he explained to me that our signature sound sits at the core of our physical body around the area of our upper abdomen. Because this sound comes from the core of our being it reflects wholly and truly who we are. We think with integrity and we speak with integrity. Stewart describes it like a single note that goes through one side of a prism and then expands with richness and fullness when it is refracted through the other side. The simple act of finding your signature note will allow you to centre yourself and connect to your inner core through the power of your own unique voice and vibration.

Gulp! Wisdom

Your voice is your identity in sound. It tells the world, through its position, tone, resonance, energy and expression, who you are.

Stewart Pearce

Gulp! Time

Music and sound therefore not only have the power to calm your mind, allowing you to access your deeper wisdom, but also the potential to foster confidence, clarify your thinking and change your emotional mood. Used in conjunction with the other reflection strategies mentioned in this book, it will really help you to find the courage to step up to your Gulp! and stay calm and centred while you move through it.

Gulp! Practice: Synchronizing with Music

1. Know the music that manages your moods:
    - What songs, or pieces of music, really calm you down and help you unwind?
    - What songs, or pieces of music, really help you to think straight?
    - What songs, or pieces of music, really help to energize you and rev you up?
2. To help you connect to your core, spend at least fifteen minutes each day listening to music that calms you. Tie this in with breathing and presencing techniques, and you'll amplify the effect.
3. Group together your other music selections and have them to hand for the times when you need to clear your head, or find courage and strength.
4. Practise humming from the note that seems to come from your upper abdomen or solar plexus just below your heart. This allows you to access your signature note.

Strategy 5: Connecting with Nature

Gulp! Wisdom

Nature has a way of reminding us
That all things great and small,
Ebb and flow in rhythm with
The heartbeat of her call.

Gulp! Time

The effectiveness of all the other centring techniques can be amplified exponentially when you reconnect with nature.

Being born and bred in New Zealand, I've been blessed by the wonderful beauty of nature; from the thick native forests rich with foliage to the remote wild beaches with not a human being in sight. By extreme contrast, I've also lived in some of the biggest cities in the world; Mexico City with a population of twenty-eight million; London with a population of twelve million and Osaka with a population of seventeen million. But the energy or vibe of each place is different. The big cities are hectic and frantic compared to the tranquillity of the countryside. In particular, I love being by the sea. It clears my head, washes away my worries and brings a sense of calm and harmony to my whole being. There is a fantastic walk on the Isle of Wight, where I go for inspiration. It is a place called Tennyson Walk, named after the poet Lord Tennyson, who lived there for many years. Walking along the cliff top I am cleansed by the winds that blow off the sea and my eyes feast on the endless horizon where sea meets sky. In this place I feel fully alive. Not only can I see my Gulp! more clearly, but experiencing the ebb and flow of nature helps me realize that I'll get through this, just like I've got through all the other challenges. I will survive. And any pain along the way will go in time. The way forward becomes clearer and I feel stronger. I leave feeling invigorated and energized, ready to take the steps I know I need to take.

This is the power of nature.

Centuries ago, we lived and died by the whims of nature. We were part of nature and she was an integral part of us. Life was simpler. Our needs were simpler. And the challenges we faced were more about life or death. These days with the urbanization of society, many of us have lost touch with nature, and the important teachings she brings. In fact, by 2007, over fifty per cent of the world's population (all 6.5 billion people of us) will live in cities and towns according to a report by the UN Commission on Population and Development. This is a huge hike up from the 1950s when only thirty per cent of the world's population lived in urban areas.

The more we urbanize, the more we try to control nature. We spend more and more time indoors, in controlled environments where the air is often processed. The little 'green' we see is also controlled and managed, often artificially fertilized to look green. It is no surprise, therefore, that we are losing our natural connection with nature. That is, until she cracks her whip and sends us reminders in the form of tsunamis like the one that hit Asia in 2004, and of course Hurricane Katrina which left mayhem in her wake as she ripped through the southern US coast in 2005.

This is the force of nature.

Michael Cohen, an ecopsychologist, has spent over sixty years as an Outdoor and Environmental Educator, and is the author of over ten books on this subject, including *Reconnecting With Nature.*[10] In his seventy-fifth year, he lives on San Juan Island, and continues to sleep outdoors throughout the seasons and make his daily hike up Mount Young. Michael is the founder of Project Nature Connect, a non-profit, special NGO consultant to the United Nations Economic and Social Council. The aim of this programme is to help people reconnect with nature and tap into nature's balance, grace and restorative powers. The fact that we spend ninety-five per cent of our time separated from nature means that we have disconnected our thinking from being sensitive to how natural systems work within us and around us. We have also become increasingly disassociated from our natural senses, and use artificial means to keep them satisfied. 'As a child, instinctively, like most children, I felt more alive, free and happy in a natural area than indoors. More intelligent, too,' recalled Michael, as we spoke over the phone. And as if on cue, we were joined by a chorus of song from two ospreys sitting on his television aerial in the background. 'With my friends, I grew up and was educated in the indoor box world of contemporary society. It detached our psyche from genuine contact with its biological origins in nature's joy, wisdom and balance.'

This phenomenon of separation and the city is not a new one. In 1854, Chief Seattle made a famous speech[11] to President Franklin Pierce who asked to purchase two million acres of land. One version of his speech has this beautiful passage:

'Our ways are different than your ways. The sight of your cities pains the eyes of the red man. There is no quiet place in the white man's cities. No place to hear the unfurling of leaves in spring or the rustle of the insect's wings. The clatter only seems to

insult the ears. And what is there to life if a man cannot hear the lonely cry of the whippoorwill or the arguments of the frogs around the pond at night? I am a red man and do not understand. The Indian prefers the soft sound of the wind darting over the face of a pond and the smell of the wind itself, cleaned by a midday rain, or scented with pinon pine.'

Think about it. How often have you actually *smelt* the wind, or even *noticed* it for that matter, except of course when it's so strong it turns your umbrella inside out. We have a plethora of natural senses that we're just not using any more, because our senses have been dulled for so long by artificial means. Spend the day by the seaside or on the top of a mountain, and you'll physically feel more alive, more vibrant and more expansive and 'whole'. You know you will, you've felt it. Return to the city and you'll physically feel yourself shrink as your senses shut down because they've been bombarded with the noise of traffic and the fume fuelled smell of the city. What's sad is that we get so used to surviving in the city, that we *forget* what it feels like to be fully alive, with all our senses open.

As you step up and Gulp!, would you rather be stressed and frantic, or fully alive and vibrant?

Drawing on the work of researcher Guy Murchie who identified over eighty different biological senses/sensitivities which pervade the natural world, Michael Cohen has identified fifty-three different ways of sensing. By opening up these senses and being aware of them, you can access much more information about your situation. What's more, when you are more conscious of being in tune with the essence of nature, you'll start to see your Gulp! from a more 'wholistic' viewpoint.

'Taking a walk in the park can clear your head for a

while,' Michael points out, 'But when you leave it doesn't take very long before you go back to being disconnected. Then you end up with the same problems because your mind remains disconnected and so the choices you make are from this closeted mind place.'

So how can you truly evaluate a problem or a challenge when you are only using a limited number of senses to evaluate it? Nature triggers more senses, and her power is twofold. First, being in the natural environment with its fresh and relatively uncontaminated energy can help to rebalance your body and clear your head so that you think more clearly. Secondly, nature is a natural system. Everything supports everything else. In nature there is never any garbage, because everything is transformed into something else that then goes back and supports the system. So tuning into nature as a system can really help you assess your challenge from a bigger 'wholistic' perspective. That means expanding your viewpoint from the symptoms of your current Gulp! and looking at it from nature's perspective. Your Gulp! is part of a bigger natural system, one that impacts both you and others. In this way, nature can 'speak' to you, triggering new insights you were completely oblivious to in your conscious mind.

So how do you do it?

'Just go to a park or an area of nature and look around,' recommends Michael. 'Look for something that attracts you and is attractive to you. Ask permission to work with it. Give it at least ten seconds to make sure the attraction is holding. Bring it into consciousness, and then let your senses do the thinking. Notice what attracts you; is it the colour? The texture? The shape? The way it sits in your hand? The smell? What do these sensations prompt you to think of? It might take time for the meaning to seep through your conscious mind. But work with it and keep looking for what's attractive.'

If something is attractive to you, it's because there is some sort of fulfilment or meaning in it for you. Michael goes on to explain that the messages that you get bring new light to the information you already have. Integrating it gives you a new reality to work from, or a different perspective or a new way of describing things. Adding the rational to what your other senses are saying helps to make it whole.

What I found so insightful about Michael's approach was that while I knew that being in nature really relaxed me and helped clear my head, I realized I was still doing it from a place of disconnection. I was 'in' nature, but not consciously 'connecting' to nature. A few days later I was at the beach and was a lot more conscious of connecting with nature. As I was walking along the shore I came upon a big pile of sandy coloured pebbles. There were hundreds of them. But one in particular stood out, so I bent down and picked it up. The first thing I noticed was how beautifully it fitted in my hand. Then I noticed how smooth and round it was on one side, yet turning it over I could see that the other side was cut, as if it had been once a whole pebble cut in half. Then I noticed the colour of the pebble, a beautiful sandy colour and the inner half of the pebble had different shades, like the insides of an ancient tree. I tried to think about what it all meant, but nothing came to me. So I popped it in my pocket and promptly forgot about it. Days later when I was at home, I found it again. And what I noticed immediately this time was the shape. It was in the shape of a heart. Then the significance came flooding to me. It reminded me that I was getting older, and while I was successful in some areas of my life, in the matters of the heart I was quite lax. Holding the pebble in my hand, I felt a deep ache, a profound yearning inside. And I knew in that moment, it was time to find my other half, my soul mate.

This is the magic of nature.

As you 'think' about the Gulp! you are facing you're doing it from the conscious mind based on information coming in from what you see, hear or feel. But what would it be like to be able to 'think' based on information from over fifty-three different senses? Now wouldn't that expand your perspective! And on top of that, wouldn't it be great to be able to tune in to nature and the essence of natural systems, and just intuitively 'get' what's really going on with you and your challenge. When Frances was facing a life-changing Gulp!, her pivot point came when she was sitting on the beach watching the waves come in and go out. In that moment she had the realization that just like the waves that come in and go out every day, she was going to get through this Gulp! and that she was going to be okay.

And I'm embarrassed to add that I never asked the pebble for permission to take it with me. That reminds me of how I, like millions of other human beings, have become so used to 'taking' what I want from nature. Now when I hold the pebble, I sense a real yearning for the sea. And I wonder, is that about me, or is that the pebble yearning to return to its resting place?

Gulp! Practice: Connecting with Nature

1. Take some time out today to be outside in nature, whether it's sitting in the park, or in your back garden, or in the hills or by the sea.
2. Just sit and observe. Notice what you find attractive. Ask permission to work with it.
3. Tune into what you find attractive and notice what attracts you to it.
4. Reflect upon what meaning this might have for the challenge you're facing.
5. Let your mind mull over this new information and write about any fresh insights in your journal over the coming days.

Gulp! Day 3 Summary: Centre & Connect

The five things to remember:

1. Silencing the chit chat of the mind allows you to connect back to your inner core and gives you access to deeper wisdom.
2. At any point in time, there is only the present moment. The past is over. The future has yet to be created.
3. Silence, stillness and natural breathing calm the mind and create space for new insights, ideas and creativity to emerge.
4. Use the harmonics of music, sound and voice to find inner calm, to organize your thoughts and to manage your moods.
5. Being in nature activates all your senses, triggering greater insights and leaving you feeling fully alive and fully connected.

Gulp! Action Plan: Centre & Connect

Starting from today, the ways in which I'm going to regularly practise centring and connecting are:

1. ______________________________

2. ______________________________

3. ______________________________

After each centring session, I'm going to reflect upon the follow questions and write down my thoughts in my journal:

What is most important to me right now?

____

What is the truth here?

____

What are my heart and soul yearning for?

____

What is my true nature calling me to do?

____

In the heat of the moment, if I need to stop and centre myself quickly, then I will do that by:

____

____

____

____

Gulp! Espresso

Spend at least ten minutes every day for the rest of the week having a centring session that incorporates stillness, breathing and relaxation.

Gulp! Mediano

Introduce a regular routine of daily centring sessions that includes stillness, breathing and relaxation, ideally for at least twenty minutes. Also include one centring session over the weekend somewhere in nature.

Gulp! Grande

For you it is imperative that centring sessions become integral to your daily activities. It will make your Gulp! much easier and less painful. First, start with at least twenty minutes of stillness, breathing and relaxation every day. Then I suggest that you book in a full day or a weekend retreat where you can be in nature, ideally alone, so that you can reflect and get greater inner clarity. In addition, taking long relaxing baths or regularly visiting a spa will be very beneficial.

Gulp! Wisdom Word

Quieten your mind and think of a number between 1 and 250.

Turn to pages 307–10 and find the word that relates to this number.

What new thoughts does this word spark?

Wisdom Word:

Gulp! Aims for Today

To spark new ideas and possibilities.
To ignite your spirit of adventure.
To consider new perspectives.

Gulp! Time

When you started this Gulp! process you probably had an idea of what you might do. I want you to totally reconsider that. I want you to start with a blank canvas, and completely think afresh about all the options available to you.

When you become still and centred inside you create space for new possibilities to emerge and bubble up. You become more creative. You start to think outside the box.

You start to see new possibilities. You start to understand the true potential of your current situation. Your thoughts become more positive and optimistic. You feel more energized and motivated. The actions you take are more proactive and committed. And the results you get are more positive, and when they're not what you expect, you can see them in a positive light.

We've already talked about fear in Day 2, because it's always the first stumbling block for people stepping up to their Gulp! But I believe that fear is not our worst enemy. I believe that our worst enemy is the inability to imagine that things could be different, that things don't have to be a certain way. That we do have a choice and we can choose to change the way things are. And that we are the creators of our own life. If we always follow the same script we're going to get the same results. But when we change the script, or create a new one, we propel ourselves into a completely new realm of possibilities and opportunities.

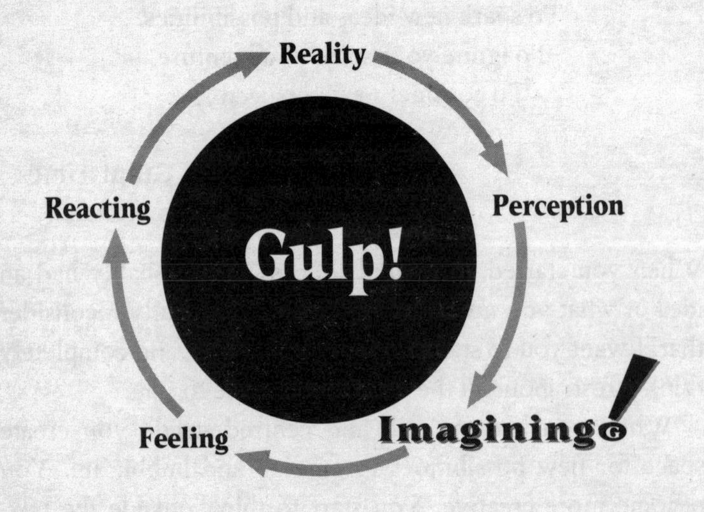

Remember The Challenge Cycle from Day 2? The aim of today is to focus on 'imagining' – simply sparking your imagination and expanding your perspective about all the options that are available to you as you face your Gulp!. My clients know this phase well; I call it 'stirring the soup of creativity'. Because that's exactly what we're going to do: put all the ingredients in a pot and just stir them up. Trust me, it can be incredibly frustrating and it can be exhilarating. Don't obsess about getting to the 'right' answer straight away. Simply open your mind and see what new insights pop up. Today is about looking at your situation from a place of *possibility*. It's about expanding your vision and seeing your Gulp! from a fresh perspective. It's about brainstorming on all the different paths you could take. And finally it's about picking the path that inspires and motivates you the most.

Gulp! Wisdom

Imagination is the beginning of creation.
You imagine what you desire;
you will what you imagine;
and at last you create what you will.

George Bernard Shaw

Gulp! Time

Coming up are the Eight Creative Sparks. Promise me that you'll work through each of the exercises. Some are more provocative than others. Some of them will work better for you than others. But whatever they spark could create an essential shift in your thinking. Make sure you centre yourself and quieten your mind before each exercise and have your journal to hand as well so that you can record your insights (sometimes great insights can come and go in seconds).

Above all, today is about having fun!

Before we start, I'd just like to get you into a good expansive frame of mind. Take a few moments now to do this simple Creative Expansion Technique. It is a blend of a number of techniques I've learnt over the years including the work of Soleira Green mentioned later in this chapter. It is very powerful for doing creative work where you need to think outside the box and from a broader perspective.

Creative Expansion Technique

1. Sit quietly. Feel your feet firmly on the ground and your bottom on the seat.
2. Silence your thoughts.
3. Gently breathe in and breathe out.
4. As you breathe out, feel yourself, and the energy around you, expanding as if you were a giant balloon.
5. Keep expanding out as far as you can go.
6. Now smile and spend a few moments thinking about someone, or something, you truly love. Feel your heart expanding and opening up.

This will put you in an expanded creative space, ideal for working through the exercises in this chapter.

Spark 1: See What 'Can Be'

Anita was frustrated in her job. She felt undervalued and unappreciated. And worse, she knew that it wasn't personal. She felt the company just didn't care about its people. She started to look around for another job, a similar position in a different company. But little did she know that twelve months down the track she would be running her own home accessories and gifts business having created her own unique range under her own brand, 'Heart and Home'.

'One day I was sitting in my cubicle and I remember thinking, "This is not what I'm meant to be doing for the rest of my life," ' recalls Anita. 'It was clear to me that the morals and values of the company just weren't the same as mine. And it got to the point where I couldn't pretend any more.'

The big problem for Anita, though, was that she didn't know what she *did* want to do for the rest of her life. That's when she came to me for coaching, to help her find out what she was meant to be doing with her career. Through the coaching, it became clearer that Anita's passion lay in retail and that she was really good at choosing gifts for people. So in the first few months we tried lots of things. We looked at what she was really good at, what she enjoyed doing and what she'd like to do if money was no object.

'Every idea came back to the issue of money,' remembers Anita. 'I found that everything that I'd like to do would mean taking a pay cut. And I didn't want to take the risk and the drop in pay.' Her light bulb moment came when I asked her to imagine she was driving down a road and there was a billboard with her very own message on it. Her reply flummoxed me, especially after all the fishing around we'd done. 'That's easy!' said Anita. 'It would be an ad for my shop.' At this point I have to admit that I was a bit stunned and had to ask, 'Er, what shop?' And then Anita proceeded to tell me about her long-standing dream to have a shop where she was selling her own range of home accessories and gifts. It was a breakthrough moment. The irony was that it had been there all along. Anita's homework was to go away and put together a Vision Board, by cutting out pictures from magazines that represented her vision. Anita came back with a complete store layout!

'As I created the Vision Board, it became so clear for me,' said Anita. 'But then I kept saying to myself "this is a stupid idea," because quite frankly I'd never wanted to work for myself. My family have their own newsagents, stationery and motel businesses, and I'd seen how they'd given their whole life to it. I like the fact that if I was ill I'd get paid, or if I wanted to go on holiday I was still paid. I didn't want to be trapped like that. What's more, I didn't want to spend the rest of my life standing in a shop!'

So we started to explore all the different options and came to the conclusion that Anita's talent was in choosing the stock and products and putting together the range. And that's exactly what she wanted to do. At that point, I made the suggestion that she could set up her own business. Anita's response was 'Could I?'

Anita's biggest concern was money. How was she going to survive? She was earning a good salary and she didn't want to give that up. Yet at the same time, going to work each day was becoming more and more painful. The ideal was to work part time. But that seemed impossible.

Then luck came her way. One of her colleagues had gone on maternity leave and was due back. So they teamed up and proposed that they job share. And that's how Anita found herself going part time. 'I took a week off and did absolutely nothing,' recalls Anita. 'It was an amazing feeling to get up any time I wanted, not being driven by an alarm clock, doing whatever I wanted, going out at whatever time I wanted and just being in control of my own destiny and life. It was a freedom that I hadn't had for years.' Then luck was to come her way yet again. The company was going through a period of big change, and voluntary redundancy suddenly became available. Anita grabbed it and left. 'When I left, I had choice,' remembers Anita. 'I had redundancy money and I had choice. What drives me in my life is freedom and choice. Freedom to do what I want, when I want. And choice to do what I want.' What's more, she quickly found some contract work, working three days a week and earning more than her full-time salary.

That's when Anita kicked into action and set up 'Heart and Home'. 'I really wanted a shop. I'd spent about six months researching the area where I wanted to open my shop, especially around the costs of premises, staff and stock,' says Anita. 'But I couldn't find the right shop. I'd got to the point where I thought, "this is not happening for a reason." The right shop in the right location isn't coming up and there's something that this is trying to tell me but I don't know what it is.' While she was on a short holiday with some friends and they were lying on the beach, Anita made the decision that the shop just wasn't right for her at that time. That's when 'Heart and Home' parties were born. 'At the beginning, all I could see was a shop in the traditional sense, not a shop that is open 24/7 online. Before I knew it, though, I was doing Heart and Home parties and running a website,' says Anita. 'My first party was at my friend Silvia's house. I remember getting out my stock, writing the prices on the tags, and laying everything out nicely. And I remember looking at it and everything was "just so". It was really "me". I was really proud that I'd done it. I'd had a vision and I created all this. I made it happen. My only regret is that I didn't have a camera!' recalls Anita.

When I asked Anita what she'd learnt from the experience, she said, 'In your gut you will know whether it's right to make that leap of faith, but don't let that little voice in your head stop you. And most of all have fun with it. It has been really hard work at times, and it's easy to get too serious. But get excited about the little things and have fun.'

Wise words from someone who never dreamed she would ever run her own business.

Like Anita, the Gulp! that you're facing is a call; a call for you to step to the next level of your life and your personal potential. But the fear that comes with moving into unfamiliar territory not only holds you back, it can also limit your vision of the options available to you.

Soleira Green, a global visionary and the author of *The Alchemical Coach Handbook*,[1] works with creatives, leaders, entrepreneurs and kids to develop their potential from the place of the biggest vision possible. 'Challenge always has a purpose,' says Soleira. 'What happens though, is that people get stuck on "what is", rather than "what can be". In fact, they can get so stuck on "what is" that they don't even look at "what can be". They only look at the issue and how to resolve the issue.' Soleira explains that there is always new potential bubbling underneath a challenge. Yes, you can simply resolve the issue, and yes you can live and learn from it, but often this is slow work and hard work. But when you look at a challenge as an opportunity for change, it becomes incredibly exciting. That's when you start looking at things in different ways. That's when you start creating new ways of operating. And that's when a simple challenge can turn into the potential for something new and something better. 'One of the biggest mistakes that people make is that they think they need to be ready first and then they'll take the step,' says Soleira: 'So they never take the step because they're never ready! But people underestimate themselves. We are all capable beings. When you take that first step, you open up to new possibilities, and everything you need simply flows to you.'

Gulp! Wisdom

For I dipped into the Future,
far as human eye could see;
saw the vision of the world,
and all the wonder that would be.
Alfred, Lord Tennyson, 1842

Gulp! Time

Gulp! Reflection

Think about your Gulp! for a few moments and ask yourself:

- What 'could be'?
- What am I not seeing?
- What if money wasn't an issue?
- What if I had complete freedom?
- If I had a motorway billboard that thousands of people would see, what would I have on it?

Spark 2: Ignite Your Imagination

As you face your Gulp!, it could be easy to say, 'I've got no choice'. But frankly, the number of options and possibilities available to you is only limited by the extent of your imagination. Now we all have an imagination, albeit some more vivid than others. We were all kids once, playing Cowboys and Indians with nothing more than a broomstick and a banana in our pocket. We've all made great mansions where they serve high tea and scones, with nothing more than a few cushions, a box, a blanket and mum's old tea set. This is the power of the imagination; the incredible human quality of being able to see something that doesn't actually exist. This is the gift of the human mind; the ability to look into the unknown and imagine what could be possible.

It takes bravery and a pioneering spirit to do this. Maybe this Gulp! you're facing is the perfect catalyst for making a dramatic change in your life. Yes you can just swim about in the pond of current choices that you know about. Or you could take a dip in the ocean of possibilities, ones that you're not even aware of . . . yet.

Take Leonardo da Vinci, the fifteenth-century painter, mathematician and engineer, for example. He was a truly inspirational genius who could look into the unknown and see possibilities that were completely radical for his time. Of the aeroplane he said, 'There shall be wings! If the accomplishment be not for me, 'tis for some other. The spirit cannot die; and man, who shall know all, shall have wings.' Not achieved during his lifetime, the 'some other' proved to be Orville and Wilbur Wright of Dayton Ohio, who would fly the first aeroplane one gusty morning in December 1903. Ironically, people around the world still did not believe it was possible to have a flying machine. Even the United States government declined their first offer of world rights on all their patents. In the face of scepticism, it wasn't until the Wright brothers[2] gave their first public displays in 1908 in Paris and Fort Myer, US, that people could 'see' it for themselves. The crowds could hardly believe their eyes. Theodore Roosevelt Jr was reported to have said, 'The crowd's gasp of astonishment was not alone at the wonder of it, but because it was so unexpected.' The rest, as they say, is history. What was merely a figment of da Vinci's imagination five centuries ago became a reality only a hundred years ago. And today, of course, what was revolutionary a hundred years ago is now an integral thread of modern-day life. In the words of Robert Goddard, hailed as the father of modern rocketry, 'It is difficult to say what is impossible, for the dream of yesterday is the hope of today and reality of tomorrow.'

So today I'd like you to find ways to simply stimulate your imagination so that you can open your mind to receiving sparks of inspiration. This can be a challenge in itself, as our multitude of senses have become so dulled by the stimuli of modern-day society.

Gulp! Reflection

Think about the Gulp! that you're facing, and then work through this three-step process aimed at sparking your imagination.

Step 1: Set the intention to open yourself to new ideas and new views.

Step 2: Visit a creative place or natural space and notice what you're attracted to or drawn to.

Step 3: Notice what fresh insights it sparks in relation to your situation. Ask yourself:

- What does this object/movement/sound/colour say about my solution?
- How does it symbolize my ideal outcome?
- If it could speak to me and give me advice, what would it say?

Ideas for creative places and natural spaces include:

1. An art gallery or photo exhibition.
2. The theatre or a movie.
3. A concert or opera.
4. A children's playground.
5. A park, a garden or the seaside.
6. A dance class.
7. Trying a new hobby, like photography, knitting, painting.

What makes these places special is that you're drawn into the vibe of creative expression. Being amongst others who are in a creative state helps you to be more creative in your own thinking. On top of that, the art form can 'speak to you' through your senses in the form of sight, sound, texture and smell, triggering fresh insights.

> **Gulp! Wisdom**
>
> A man's mind stretched by a new experience,
> can never go back to its old dimensions.
> *Oliver Wendell Holmes Jr*
>
> **Gulp! Time**

Spark 3: Challenge the Status Quo

For many of my clients, one of their biggest obstacles when they step up to their challenge is going against the family and cultural norms. This can be the hardest decision to make. What do you do when your heart and soul are calling you one way, yet the 'culture and clan' are pulling you another? What do you do? Follow your heart and inner wisdom and risk alienation? Or conform to the norm and feel your spirit wither away? For most people there is always some middle ground. But it takes a brave soul to challenge the status quo and risk disappointing the people around you.

History is full of amazing people who have challenged the status quo, imagining new possibilities completely outside the box and changing the course of the world in the process. They have created what we call a 'paradigm shift' in society, a fundamental change in underlying beliefs that drive our culture. Most of them are ordinary people who have achieved extraordinary things, simply because they were prepared to challenge the status quo. Here are some of them:

- **Kate Sheppard,** born Catherine Wilson Malcolm in Liverpool in 1847, went on to champion women's rights in New Zealand, making it the first nation in the world to grant women full voting rights in 1893.

- **Marya Sklodowska,** born in Warsaw on 7 November 1867, married Pierre Curie. While battling sexism in science she and her husband went on to discover radium and radioactivity.
- **Mohandas Karamchand Gandhi** was born on 2 October 1869 in Porbandar, western India. He went on to lead the Indian people in overthrowing British colonization, using a philosophy of peace and non-violence.
- **Rosa Louise McCauley Parks** was born on 4 February 1913 in Tuskegee, Alabama. On 1 December 1955, a bus driver ordered her to give up her seat to a white man. She refused and was fined. The bus boycott that ensued was to propel the civil rights movement led by Martin Luther King.
- **Nelson Rolihlahla Mandela** was born in a village near Umtata in the Transkei on 18 July 1918. After spending over eighteen years in Robben Island prison, driven by a passionate vision of a free South Africa, he led the people to bring an end to apartheid.
- Born on 28 October 1955 in Seattle, **William (Bill) H. Gates,** guided by his vision that there could be a PC in every home (an incredible thought at the time), has revolutionized the world with his personal computing software.

These people are pioneers. Each and every one of them had to swim against the tide of social norm. But each had an inner drive that kept them going, fuelled by a passion for what they believed in, and a higher vision that things could be different. Through their resolve, their commitment and their ability to imagine the impossible, they were able to share their vision, Gulp! and shine a light on the way forward for others. They were able to paint a picture of a new ideal. And over time, their simple acts were enough to change the consciousness of society, paving the way for a whole new belief paradigm and a whole new concept of 'the norm'.

I believe that Ellen MacArthur[3] is one of the great 'paradigm shifters' of this decade. For over two months she lived alone on the *B&Q*, a multihull boat that measured seventy-five feet long by fifty feet wide with a mast ninety feet high. Single-handedly she dealt with the daily dilemmas of mountainous seas, icebergs and gale force winds and she narrowly missed a collision with a whale. Living conditions were basic. It was all about survival. Food was freeze dried. Sleep was scarce with twenty-minute naps throughout the day, when she got the chance. And as for luxuries . . . there was no loo ('just bucket and chuck it') and no shower.

On 7 February 2005, after seventy-one days at sea alone, she crossed the finish line to break the world record for circumnavigating the world solo. In her book *Race Against Time*, Ellen says, '*You have to believe you have a chance when you start on something like this. You have to believe that you can do it.*' Her Nan got a degree at eighty-four and she inspired her to never give up if you really want something.

When Ellen MacArthur sailed across the finish line, she created a paradigm shift in the world, a fundamental change in underlying beliefs. Until then, let's face it, most of us would have imagined that the fastest sailor to circumnavigate the globe single-handedly would more than likely be a man in his late thirties with an overgrown beard and a broad muscular chest. When she crossed the finish line, Ellen defied all stereotypes. She's female. She was twenty-eight. And she only stands at five feet three! Who would have ever predicted that she would be the fastest person ever to sail solo around the world? The truth is, like the tale of the Wright brothers, if we hadn't seen it for ourselves, none of us would have believed it.

It really makes you think. If she can do that, what else can she do?

And it makes you think, doesn't it . . . if she can do that, what else could *we* be doing?

For me, tucking into my Christmas dinner while she was out there on the high seas battling with sails and climbing ninety-foot masts, it made me challenge all my own assumptions about . . . being too old, being a woman, being too tall, being from a little country down under. All the beliefs that have held me back from even attempting things that might challenge me. Her feats inspired me to think outside the realm of 'reality', and imagine what 'could be' if I let go of my own beliefs that were holding me back.

This is the power of a paradigm shift.

Gulp! Reflection

Spend a few moments now to reflect upon the challenge you're facing:

- What excuses are you making up?
- If you were to follow 'the norm', what decision would you make?
- If you were to go completely against 'the norm', what decision would you make?

- What scares you about challenging the status quo?
- What inspires you about challenging the status quo?

Spark 4: Embrace the Spirit of Adventure

Gulp! Wisdom

Twenty years from now you will be more
disappointed by the things
you didn't do than by the ones you did do.
So throw off the bowlines,
Sail away from the safe harbour.
Catch the trade winds in your sails.
Explore. Dream. Discover.
Mark Twain

Gulp! Time

This is a fabulous quote from Mark Twain, which beautifully encapsulates the spirit of adventure. Yet why do we lose sight of our pioneering spirit? I remember distinctly a conversation with a guy I worked with in Mexico. He had had a near death experience when he almost drowned one day in the sea. He recalled everything slowing down and his life literally passing before him. He also saw the bright light that is so often spoken of, and experienced an incredible sense of calm. What was interesting is that the meaning of his life suddenly became apparent, and he remembers smiling at the simplicity of it. When he was later resuscitated, he couldn't remember what it was. But the experience left an indelible impact on him. Since then he is supremely conscious of the gift that life is. He makes a point of incorporating exciting adventures into his life like skydiving and travelling to exotic places.

But why is it that we need to have these wake-up calls to really appreciate the wonder that life holds for us? For me, it took finding The Lump in my breast and the threat of cancer to kickstart my writing career. The choice was always there, but it took a 'now or never' situation to provide the impetus to do something about it.

The Oxford English Dictionary defines 'adventure' as '*an unusual, exciting, and daring experience*'. Just think for a moment about the last time you had one of those? Hopefully you don't have to think too hard. But for many of us, the adventures have been few and far between. Somehow we get stuck in living our lives, and because we're 'in' them it's difficult to see how narrow they've become. Reigniting your spirit of adventure will not only bring fresh energy, it'll also give you a more adventurous perspective for the challenge that you're facing.

Recently I heard Judy Leden,[4] one of the world's greatest hang-gliders, speak about her exciting adventures. For someone who had a fear of heights, her adventures are absolutely mind blowing. As she says in her book *Flying With Condors*, '*When you are putting your life on the line, and you know that it's minus 87 degrees and that, if your oxygen fails, you have 45 seconds to live, it enhances all your senses.*' Her flying feats include hang-gliding from the summit of one of the world's highest active volcanoes, flying a microlight plane all the way from England to the Kingdom of Jordan, and beating the World Altitude Record by jumping from a balloon. Her talk was about the latter and she showed some amazing video footage. It was one of her most dangerous projects, her aim being to break the World Altitude Record, which had been set in 1984. So on 25 October 1994 in Amman, she, in her hang-glider attached to a balloon, ascended 38,900 feet above the earth's surface. Then, with one snip, they cut the line between her glider and the balloon, propelling her into freefall. This specific moment was captured on the video and I remember the whole room gasping, as we felt *ourselves* going into freefall. Judy's journey ended two hours later, her flesh and her eyelids freezing with frostbite, landing back on earth and taking the world altitude record.

Now life is all about contrasts, and while this isn't something I would do myself, it clearly demonstrates courage, risk and sheer determination. It got me thinking. Where am I playing it safe? Where in my life could I take a few more risks? If I looked at my Gulp! from a place of adventure, what would I do?

Gulp! Reflection

Think about your Gulp! situation:

- What would be the most adventurous thing to do?
- What would be the riskiest solution?
- What would be the most daring thing to do?

Spark 5: See Things Differently

When both her children started school Louise decided it was time to return to work. She'd had a very successful career in PR and was really looking forward to getting back to the buzz of the media world. But she was afraid. She'd been out of the industry for over seven years. Maybe she was too rusty. Maybe she'd lost her touch. Would she be able to cut it with all the younger talent moving up the ranks? When Louise started to look at her situation from different perspectives, she realized that being out of the industry for the last seven years didn't have to be a disadvantage. First, she would be the ideal person to work for clients targeting young mothers or children. Secondly, she was brimming with new ideas on smart ways to get PR, ones that were innovative and outside the box. And thirdly, with all the multi-tasking that comes from managing a household, she realized her management skills were streets ahead of what they ever used to be when she was single, footloose and fancy free. This switch in perspective left Louise feeling more confident and sure of her own ability. Of course this came across in her interviews and she was quickly snapped up.

The interesting thing about perspective is that we get stuck looking at our Gulp! from a certain, and often fixed, viewpoint. Yet when we look at it from a completely different angle, it can create a paradigm shift in our thinking so powerful that it puts a completely different spin on our Gulp!, opening the door for a whole new range of options to emerge. They were always there. It's just that we didn't see them. It's like getting a new pair of glasses. Suddenly you see things differently.

Experiencing other cultures always opens my eyes to new ways of thinking. And it shows me the rich diversity that we have within the human race. In my lifetime, I've lived in New Zealand, Japan, France, Mexico and England, and visited many more countries in my globetrotting travels. Time and time again, it's made me realize that the way I think and the way I was brought up is only one perspective of the world; there are so many other different viewpoints.

I distinctly recall the time I was living in Mexico working

for a multinational market research company. They had a big world map on the wall in their reception area. The first time I saw it, I was horrified. Not only was New Zealand in a corner way down on the bottom left, they'd cut half the North Island off! I spoke to the receptionist about this, and explained ever so nicely that New Zealand should be in the middle of the map. She looked at me bemused. I explained again, even more patiently, that in world maps New Zealand was always right there in the middle. Her reply dumbfounded me. She explained that in Mexico, the world maps had Mexico right bang in the centre. I was astonished. All my life, New Zealand had always been in the centre of the world map. In fact my view of how the world is laid out comes from this perspective. But when you put another country in the middle it completely changes the way the world actually looks.

In my travels there have been many examples like this, that challenge my whole belief system of how things 'should' be. I've realized that we are products of our cultures. Our thinking is shaped by our culture and our upbringing. And more often than not we don't even know it. Until of course you experience a different culture and see that things are done differently. This contrast is great for questioning your own assumptions about life, especially the ones you take for granted. Take, for example, slurping your noodles. In England, slurping your noodles would get you a disapproving stare from your mother. But in Japan, having a good slurp of your udon would show appreciation, getting you beaming looks of approval from your host.

There never is only one way. And there is no right or wrong way. We just see things differently.

So when you look at stepping up to your Gulp!, what

viewpoint are you taking? What mindset are you using? If you were to turn things on their head, what would your Gulp! look like?

Gulp! Wisdom

Think left and think right and think low
and think high.
Oh, the thinks you can think up if only you try!
Dr Seuss

Gulp! Time

Here's a quick exercise for you.

Gulp! Reflection

Think about your Gulp! for a moment.

- If you took the perspective of **fun,** what choices would you make?
- If you took the perspective of **easy,** what actions would you take?
- If you turned your Gulp! **upside down,** how would you describe it?
- If you considered the **best case** what would happen?
- If you picked a **different perspective**, what would it be?

Spark 6: Rewrite Your Beliefs

One day when Jean was washing her hair, as she leaned over the bath she suddenly felt this strange tender lump in her left breast. She was shocked, and immediately thought of her mother, who had had breast cancer and died seven years later. Feeling apprehensive she went straight to the doctor. Her fears were confirmed. She had cancer. 'It was more a shock to find the lump rather than a shock to be told it was cancerous,' recalls Jean. Her mother and four cousins had all suffered from breast cancer. So how did Jean deal with it? 'They always say be positive,' says Jean. 'I think I was positive, I decided I was going to get better. I was going to be all right.' And she was, and still is today.

Henry Ford famously said, 'If you think you can do a thing, or if you think you can't do a thing, you're right.' Our fundamental beliefs drive our thinking. And as you know from Day 2, what we think influences what we can imagine, which in turn becomes the impetus for what we're feeling and what actions we take.

Gulp! Wisdom

Your inner landscape paints your outer landscape.

Gulp! Time

If you think stepping up to your Gulp! is going to be hard, guess what? It will be hard. If you think it will be easy, then you'll find it *is* a lot easier than you think. Most of our beliefs find their roots in our family beliefs which are heavily influenced by our cultural beliefs. It is these core beliefs that can create prison bars around our mind. And challenging these beliefs can feel a bit like wading upstream against the current of the river. They are often very ingrained in us, and it takes courage to challenge them and then choose to think differently about them.

Take these sayings, for example, that encapsulate some core beliefs:

- 'No pain, no gain.'
- 'All good things must come to an end.'
- 'Easier said than done.'
- 'All good things come to those who wait.'
- 'Curiosity killed the cat.'
- 'Seeking happiness is a straight way to misery.'
- 'Great trees keep down little ones.'

It's not surprising if just reading this list makes you begin to feel gloomy and depressed. Why bother making your Gulp! at all? You're only going be miserable, be in pain or die. As you know from Day 2, our feelings are the crucial link between our thoughts and actions. So if you feel gloomy and can't be bothered, then your actions will reflect this.

Many of these sayings were created in times when things were physically tough. Are they truly relevant any more?

Just by changing *one* word in each saying, they can have a completely different sense and meaning. Look at the difference it makes.

- 'No pain, *big* gain.'
- 'All good things must come *from* an end.'
- 'Easier said, *easier* done.'
- 'All good things come to those who *whistle*.'
- 'Curiosity *created* the cat.'
- 'Seeking happiness is a straight way *from* misery.'
- 'Great trees keep *up* little ones.'

Say these out aloud. At first they sound peculiar. Notice how odd they feel, how they just don't feel 'right'. But who says you can't have gain without any pain? Who says being curious has to lead to demise? And who says all good things have to come to an end? Why can't they lead to new beginnings?

At the same time, the more you read these new versions, the more part of you *can* relate to them. Part of you *can* remember times when you gained something without any pain. Part of you *does* recall a time when you thought things would be easy and they were.

So both versions hold truth. But as you face your Gulp!, which perspective will you choose to take? Which beliefs will you use to guide your thinking? Once again, there is no right or wrong. There is just what you believe to be true. This perspective greatly influences the way you approach your Gulp!, which will in turn affect the outcome you get.

These are some of the common beliefs that hold people back from making their Gulp!:

- I'm not good enough.
- I'm too old/young/fat/thin/short/tall.
- I don't deserve it.
- I'm not important.
- I'm not strong/smart/brave/clever enough.

Imagine for a minute facing your challenge from any one of these perspectives. What would you do and what would be the likely outcome?

Rewriting your beliefs is easy. It's believing in them that can be the hard part.

Gulp! Reflection

Think about the challenge you're facing:

- What core beliefs are holding *you* back?
  (e.g. I'm not smart enough.)
- Then flip it and write down the opposite of each one of those beliefs.
  (e.g. I **am** *smart enough.)*
- Now think about at least one example in your lifetime that proves that each of these beliefs can be true.
  (e.g. I have a university degree, which proves I can learn.)
- Pick the three beliefs that are most important for you to have as you step up to your challenge. Write them on a Post-It note and put them where you can see them every day.

Spark 7: Invent New Possibilities

Sometimes when your back is against the wall and you think there is no way out, it can motivate you to dig deep and come up with a truly inventive solution. That's because none of the current ones seem to be working for you. As Albert Einstein once said, 'Necessity is the mother of invention'.

Some of the world's greatest inventions have come from the spark of someone's imagination in the face of challenge and adversity. These people were in challenging Gulp! situations and yet had the ability to see that things *could* be different and that there *could* be a better way.

- **Anita Roddick**[5] started the Body Shop in 1976 in Littlehampton, to create a livelihood for herself and her two daughters, when her husband was trekking across the Americas.

- In 1873, young **Chester Greenwood**, aged 15, trudged an eight-mile route selling eggs from house to house to help put food on the family table. He invented the world's first earmuffs to keep his ears warm.
- In 1897, **Felix Hoffmann** was desperately searching for something to relieve his father's excruciatingly painful arthritis. He studied the experiments of Charles Gergardt (a French chemist) and 'rediscovered' acetylsalicylic acid – or aspirin, as we know it today.
- Recently divorced, unemployed and struggling for money, **J.K. Rowling** wrote the first magical story of Harry Potter huddled in a restaurant so she and her baby daughter could keep warm.

There is nothing like staring adversity in the face to spark new thinking and to awaken new courses of action.

- When Claire's husband left her for a younger woman, she was traumatized. They'd been married for twenty years and she'd stuck by him through some pretty tough times. After a period of shock and deep mourning, she started to rekindle her passion for acting, took acting classes and started to piece her life back together.
- When Paul was passed over for promotion yet again, he was furious. Despite putting in the long hours and producing good quality work, he was told that he 'wasn't quite there yet'. So he hired a coach and worked on his personal impact and leadership abilities. He was promoted within six months.
- When Jane lost her baby she was devastated. They'd

tried for months, and had been over the moon when she finally became pregnant. The shock of it really made her look at her lifestyle. She stopped smoking, started going to the gym and introduced organic food into her diet. She is fitter, healthier and more vibrant than she's ever been, and they're trying for another baby.

Luckily, you don't always have to wait for a traumatic situation to arise to be inventive. Despite what you might be thinking right now, there are limitless opportunities and possibilities open to you right now. But more often than not, we get stuck in one perspective and see only a few options. Being inventive is about thinking of all sorts of possible outcomes, from the sublime to the ridiculous. By doing this you broaden your thinking and create a wide range of different scenarios. It is the breadth of this range that is powerful. The more contrast you create between the ideas, the clearer you get about what course of action you want to take. It also soothes the mind because you realize that there is more than one path you can take. You have options. You have choice. And this brings with it a strong sense of empowerment.

The Wheel of Possibilities is a great way of brainstorming all the different options available to you and it's great for sparking new ideas, ones that you might not have thought of before.

- First, draw a small circle in the middle and put 'me' in the centre. Just in case you've forgotten, you are the creator in your life and at the centre of all the decisions you make.
- Secondly, draw a number of spokes out from the inner circle, and at the end of each of these, write down a different possibility or outcome.

- Thirdly, rate how inspired you feel by each option on a scale of zero to ten, where zero is at the centre of the wheel and ten is the outer rim.
- Fourthly, sit back and reflect upon the different options. Notice what you think and feel.

Wheel of Possibilities

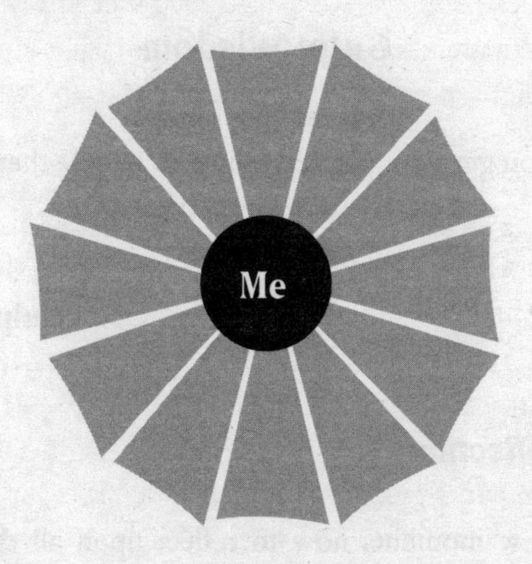

Nick tried this exercise when he was tired of living in the city. Now that he was self-employed with his own internet business he could work anywhere in the world. Initially, he thought of getting a small flat somewhere by the sea. But the more he thought about it, the more he realized that he'd rather live permanently by the sea. When I asked him to invent twelve different scenarios, he came up with over twenty different options, some of them getting a bit wild and wacky. What he found useful was that by laying all his cards on the table, he could get a better sense of what he 'felt' was the best option, the best course of action. What became apparent to him while he was doing the rating was that while he did want to move to the seaside, he didn't want it to negatively impact his business. In the end he chose to rent out his house in the city and rent a small apartment by the seaside with beautiful sea views for six months. This way he could evaluate the impact a permanent move would have on his internet business and on his social life.

Gulp! Wisdom

Ideas are like rabbits.
You get a couple, learn how to handle them,
and pretty soon you have a dozen.
John Steinbeck

Gulp! Time

Gulp! Reflection

Spend a few moments now to reflect upon all the options available to you:

- Create your own Wheel of Possibilities diagram.
- Write down at least twelve different possible scenarios or options. Cover the broadest range possible.
- Look at the list and carefully assess each option. Rate them from zero to ten in terms of how much they inspire you.
- Reflect upon your possibilities:
  - What makes your top three options feel better than the others?
  - What criteria underpin this selection?

Spark 8: Connect to a Higher Purpose

When you feel connected to something that is bigger than just you, there is a subtle shift in your focus. You become less concerned about what you want and more interested in what is best for the greater good. Your decisions are less narrow minded and your vista is broader and wider. You feel connected to more than just you. When you step up to your Gulp! from this place there is something magical that happens. You are aware of a bigger picture and can put into perspective what is happening to you in the context of a greater plan. When this happens, what you find is that you're driven by different motivations and you focus not only on what is best for you, but on what the greater good is calling you to do. This is not about making sacrifices or putting what others want ahead of your own needs. This is about seeing your Gulp! from the perspective of the greater good, something that is bigger than just you. In this way you become a contributor. Rather than making the Gulp! just for yourself, you're doing it for others as well.

People can get an incredible strength from approaching a Gulp! from this perspective. When Petra's boss shouted at her in front of her team, it was the last straw. Her boss was well known for being aggressive and it was widely accepted that that 'was just his style', even by Human Resources, despite the fact that most of his direct reports had moved on within a year. Petra had been loyal, and always focused on her boss's good qualities. But ripping into her in front of her team in an open plan office was pushing it too far. So she decided to speak to him about his behaviour. Despite the fact that she was petrified of losing her job or being shouted at again, Petra looked around her at the talented people that worked in his department. She knew that the business would lose many of these people if the boss's behaviour wasn't addressed. In addition, it was sending the message to others that bullying behaviour was acceptable. Which it wasn't. What's more, she realized that if his behaviour didn't improve she was going to leave anyway, so she had nothing to lose. She drew great strength in knowing that by standing up to him and standing her ground, she was making a difference. If he changed his behaviour even slightly, it would benefit the whole department, both in terms of productivity and creativity. So she rehearsed what she was going to say, practised her breathing and centring techniques and finally made the Gulp! and spoke to him calmly, rationally and firmly. He was shocked. In fact he was so shocked he didn't know what to say. It was a difficult conversation for both of them. And when Petra left his office she was shaking. His behaviour did improve, albeit slowly, but he never shouted at her again in front of her team.

There is an incredible power in working with others to create change. This is how movements happen. The power of the collective is greater than the power of the individual. When everyone is heading in the same direction, you're all contributing to a vision that is bigger than any one of you. This brings with it an impetus and momentum that can be extraordinary. It is like a wave that gathers momentum and size on its way to the seashore. When you are stepping up to your Gulp! and you feel like you are 'in' the wave, you can ride on the momentum of the greater purpose, the collective good of everyone else involved.

Jamie Oliver[6] and his School Dinners campaign is a great example of how someone steps up to the Gulp! with the greater good in mind. Passionate about food and horrified at the quality of many school dinners being tucked into by Britain's schoolkids every day, he decided to take over the canteen of a school in Greenwich with the sole aim of getting the kids eating better quality food, and keeping within the school budget – no mean feat even for a celebrity chef. What ensued was a fascinating four-part television series that uncovered the horrors of Britain's school dinners and tracked the ups and downs of his lofty mission. Others had been campaigning for better school dinners for years, but in four weeks Jamie was able to raise the consciousness of a whole nation, get government backing for changes in policy and even be asked if he'd run for Prime Minister. The cynics will only look at how much money he's made from licensing and merchandizing deals. And what I say is, good for him. It took balls to make a stand like this on national TV, especially with so many people waiting for him to fall flat on his face. As a result, millions of us are now more aware about what we're putting into the mouths of our future generation and the impact this has on their health, productivity and behaviour. And Jamie is getting paid to take this powerful message worldwide. Sounds like a win/win to me.

There is a higher purpose in the Gulp! you're facing if you look for it. That's because everything happens for a reason. And even under the most chaotic of situations, there is an underlying order, a pulse and sense of purpose.

Gulp! Wisdom

Never doubt that a small group of thoughtful,
committed citizens can change the world.
Indeed it is the only thing that ever has.
Margaret Mead

Gulp! Time

Gulp! Reflection

Think about the challenge you're facing right now.

- What statement will you be making to yourself and others?
- How is what you're doing contributing to the greater good?
- What are you being a role model for?

Gulp! Day 4 Summary: Imagine & Invent

The five things to remember:

1. The possibilities open to you are only limited by the extent of your imagination.
2. When you expand your mind your options will increase.
3. Be creative. Think outside the box and find new perspectives.
4. Your beliefs form the basis of your actions. Choose them wisely.
5. You create your own reality. So what do you want to create?

Gulp! Action Plan: Imagine & Invent

After working through the reflection exercises, the ideas that really light my fire and inspire me are:

1. ____

2. ____

3. ____

What I need to believe about myself to achieve these is that I am:

____

____

____

To make these ideas feel more real and achievable, I'm going to:

____

____

____

Here are some suggestions to help you to make your ideas more real:

Visualizing them. Just close your eyes and see if you can put yourself in the ideal situation. What do you see? What do you hear? How do you feel? Make the image as big as possible in full colour. Write about your experience in your journal.

Writing a letter to the future. Imagine that you have already achieved it, and that you are writing a letter to someone you care about. Describe to them what is happening and what you are experiencing. Write this down in your journal.

Creating a Vision Board. Simply get an old pile of magazines out and cut out pictures that represent your ideal vision. They can be any picture including abstract colours, textures and objects. Also cut out words that express how you are feeling in your vision. Paste these cut-out pictures onto a large piece of paper and sit back and reflect upon it. Write your thoughts and insights in your journal.

Mock it up. Make a physical replica of your vision. For example, if you're after a new job, mock up your new business card. Or if you are going to ask your girlfriend to marry you, mock up the wedding invitation. Put your prototype in a place where you can see it every day.

Gulp! Espresso

Imagine the ideal outcome and write it down on a Post-It note. Spend some time today daydreaming about what it would be like.

Gulp! Mediano

Spend some time today writing a letter to the future. While you're at it, reflect upon your thoughts and insights and turn them into a powerful picture in your mind. Then choose something to remind you of your vision. It can be an object, a photo, some music or even a reminder on your mobile phone. Over the coming week, spend some time conjuring up your vision at every opportunity possible. Write any new insights in your journal.

Gulp! Grande

Make a date with yourself and block at least three hours out one day this week. You'll also need some scissors, old magazines and glue. Start with a centring session. Then while you're in a relaxed state, take yourself into the future and imagine your ideal outcome. Create a strong picture in your mind and then write a letter to the future about it. When you've done that, create a Vision Board by cutting out pictures from magazines that reflect your vision. Take it a step further and create a mock-up if it's appropriate. Finally, spend at least half an hour just reflecting on what you've created today and write your thoughts and insights in your journal. Put your Vision Board in a place where you can see it on a daily basis, and reflect upon it during your centring sessions.

Gulp! Wisdom Word

Quieten your mind and think of a number between 1 and 250.

Turn to pages 307–10 and find the word that relates to this number.

What new thoughts does this word spark?

Wisdom Word:

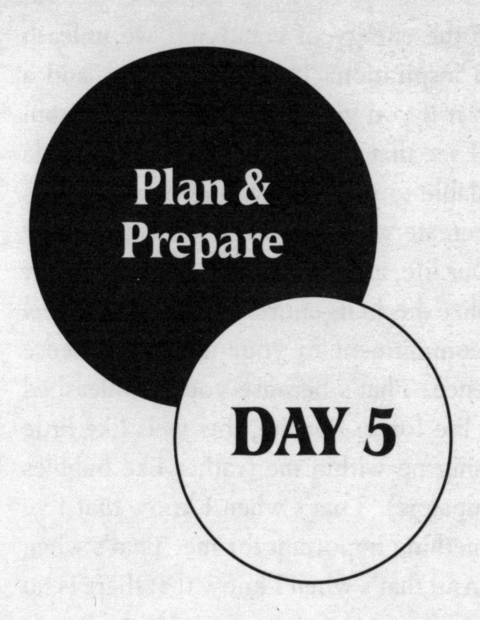

Gulp! Aims for Today

To chart your course forward.
To turn ideas into action.
To build your energy reservoir.

Gulp! Time

After stirring up the soup of creativity, you're probably overflowing with a plethora of different ideas. I hope that you can now see your Gulp! in a different light. I hope that you now consider your Gulp! as an opportunity to grow and learn and move your life to a better place. And I hope that you can now feel thankful (even just a little bit) because your Gulp! has been a catalyst for you to make some much needed changes in your life.

When we tap into the energy of creativity, we unleash fresh enthusiasm and inspiration. This brings hope, and a sense that you *can* do it if you give it your best shot. From the last chapter you'll see that there is actually a very wide range of options available to you, that you do have choices and it's up to you to create what you want to happen. You are at the centre of your life, and you are the creator of your future. When you realize this in its entirety you'll start to feel a stronger sense of commitment to your mission, a sense of surety and confidence. That's because you've unleashed your *vis vitalis*, your life force. For me, this feels like little bubbles of energy rising up within me (rather like bubbles in a glass of fine champagne). That's when I know that I've really tapped into something important for me. That's when I know I'm on track. And that's when I know that there is no going back.

Gulp!

One of the biggest challenges with all this creative energy is that you can become so inspired that you end up running around in all directions like a headless chicken. Being able to harness the bubbling enthusiasm and channelling it is a scientific art. And we've come to the point now where you need to do that and make a choice about your way forward.

Remember at the start of the book, when I talked about 'Grasshopper'? He had this innate ability to meet a challenge head on, and then swiftly and effortlessly take the appropriate action with the right timing and right on target. Then he'd return to his centre ready for the next challenge. Now that you've done the meditation and creative work, today is about getting really practical, by tuning into what's really important and focusing on preparing yourself for your big Gulp!. The whole point of connecting to your centre, building your inner strength and learning to go with the flow is so that the action phase doesn't become a flurry of meaningless and knee-jerk activity, most of which simply dissipates your energy. Instead it is about taking a more considered and tactical approach, one that spends your energy wisely, undertaking only the activities that are best to propel you forward along your chosen path. This way you save time and energy. And your Gulp! becomes easier and more effortless, with each step forward leading gracefully to the next.

Gulp! Wisdom

With each risk you take,
each time you move out of what feels comfortable,
you become more powerful.
Susan Jeffers

Gulp! Time

So today, you're going to make some clear decisions about your Gulp!. You're going to clearly define your intention and chart your course ahead. And you'll start building footbridges, planning, preparing and practising what you need to do. But in saying that, I don't want you to become too rigid about your planning and preparation. Yes, there needs to be an element of focus as you step forward, but I also want you to allow the inertia that naturally comes with the creative process to propel you forward. So it's about planning and preparing yourself without overdoing it. In the words of Napoleon Bonaparte, 'Over-preparation is the foe of inspiration.'

We're also going to explore ways in which you can prepare yourself physically for your Gulp!, by keeping your energy reservoir levels high, and by maximizing energy gainers and minimizing energy drainers. Finally, we'll take a look at some common pitfalls that are of our own making, and how we can overcome them. By the end of today, you'll be ready to take clear, tactical and decisive action and be well on your way to going for Gulp!

Charting Your Course

The first thing we'll do today is clarify where you want to go and what path you want to take. The focus of the last chapter was to expand your perspective and see what new possibilities emerged. I hope that some new insights popped through. Maybe the path you want to take now is different to the one you originally thought of when you started this process. Or maybe you're just clearer that your original thinking is the best way forward. Either way, it's time to make a choice and set a clear intention.

Gulp! Wisdom

One doesn't discover new lands
without consenting to lose sight of the shore for
a very long time.
André Gide

Gulp! Time

When it comes to planning the way forward, the Gulp! philosophy is not to plan each individual step in the process, but rather to chart the general course and then focus on simply taking the first steps. Just like the explorers in the seventeenth century who ventured out into unknown and uncharted waters with nothing but the skill and instinct of the captain and crew and the stars and wind to guide them, so too can we step forward and Gulp!.

But you need to set a clear intention and, just as importantly, you need to let go of fully controlling how you get there and learn to be in the flow.

Much has been written about the power of setting clear intentions. Real magic can happen when you set an intention that's aligned to your true nature, and when you put your heart and soul behind it. It's as if the stars align themselves around you, guiding you on your journey through the dark of the night, and the wind brings just the right force to help you navigate your way swiftly and without hitting any icebergs. Dr Wayne Dyer has written a great book about intention, aptly titled, *The Power of Intention.*[1] He says that, '*connecting to intention means listening to your heart and conducting yourself based on what your inner voice tells you is your purpose here.*' (Page 86.)

To hear your inner voice you need to be able to silence your thoughts, which is why it's such a fundamental part of the Gulp! philosophy. What I've also found to be very powerful in stepping up to any Gulp! is to take the perspective of not just *intention*, but of *creation* as well. That's because we are the creators of our own life. We create everything around us through our thoughts and feelings. We create our relationships, we create our luck and we even create our own obstacles. We are at the centre of our life, and therefore we must take responsibility for every choice we make. And when we create from the place of our inner core, what we create is pure and aligned to our truest nature. It carries the essence of love, compassion, peace and unity, and it acknowledges the universal source of all things and our innate interconnectedness to all that is.

There is a fascinating movie called *What the BLEEP! Do We Know?*[2] You might have seen it. It's not your conventional movie, rather it is a 'docudrama' that uses actors, expert interviews and animation, taking the viewer into the complex world of quantum physics to explain how we can create endless possibilities for our everyday reality. I've watched it a few times and each time I see it I 'hear' something different. But one interview has always stuck out for me. It's this one from Dr Joe Dispenza:

Gulp! Wisdom

I Create My Day

I wake up in the morning and I consciously create
my day the way I want it to happen.
When I create my day and out of nowhere little things
happen that are so unexplainable,
I know that they are the process or the result of
my creation.
And this gives me the power and the incentive to
do it the next day.

Joe Dispenza

Gulp! Time

As you face your Gulp!, put yourself at the centre of your own world, and ask yourself, 'What is it that I want to create? What is my true nature calling me to create? And how can I bring this into being and stay aligned to the purity of my true nature?'

This is why centring yourself is so important. When you can connect to your inner wisdom and create your intention from this place, then you attract the right opportunities to you and take only the action that is aligned to your true nature, rather than to the frantic whims of your ego mind.

Gulp! Wisdom

As a man thinks in his heart, so is he.

Proverbs 23:7

Gulp! Time

Remember, you are the captain of your own ship. As you embark on your Gulp! journey, you can be creating your reality every step of the way.

Creating Your Attitude

You can create how you want to feel as you step up to your Gulp!. You can create fear, or you can create hope. You can create resignation and despair or you can create anticipation and excitement. You have the choice. You are the master of your mind and your emotions. So you can create the attitude that you want.

Creating Your Obstacles

You can also go around creating obstacles for yourself. That's because your beliefs and thoughts create your reality. If you think it's going to be difficult, then invariably it will be difficult. If you think it's going to go all wrong, then invariably it will. Obstacles that crop up in your journey are simply occurrences that force you to stop, check your ego and reflect on what you're actually creating. If you follow the flow, it's rare that obstacles even get created. That's because being in the flow means you're aligned to your true nature.

Creating Your Future

As you consider your Gulp!, know that you are at the centre of what outcome is created. You are the driving force behind it. So what do you want to create? Of all the options you explored in the last chapter, what is the ideal scenario that you want to create?

Creating Your Luck

We've seen how the same situation can be perceived from different perspectives. In your current situation you can create more suffering and frustration, or you can create the chance to turn the tide and create a pivot point. You can also take advantage of all the possibilities and opportunities that actually surround you right here, right now, and create the chance for magic to happen. But you can only do this if you're awake and watching.

Gulp! Wisdom

Every day in every way I create my own reality.
So what is it that I choose to create today?

Gulp! Time

'But what about other people getting in the way or obstacles that crop up randomly in your path?' I hear you ask. 'I can't control those things.' That's true. You can't. But what you *can* do is control your reaction and response to things that crop up on your path. If you remain centred and connected you will observe the obstacles, but not become absorbed by them. As an observer, you remain detached, and that creates space for you to reflect upon what you want to create in response. Remember, you are the captain of your ship. If the wind changes you can choose which tack to take. If the night sky becomes dark and cloudy and you can't see the guiding stars, you can choose to rest or continue with your map and compass. If the cabin boy spots new land far away on the horizon, you can choose to land immediately or spend time investigating further.

So, Captain, what do you want to create?

Gulp! Reflection

As you face your Gulp!:

- What outcome do you want to create?
- What attitude do you want to create?
- What feelings do you want to have?
- What obstacles do you choose *not* to create?

Gulp! Wisdom

Luck happens when preparation meets opportunity.
Seneca

Gulp! Time

In all the research interviews I conducted, 'preparation' was one of the key secrets to success. The power of preparation comes from plugging the gaps of the unknown.

Imagine that you're on one side of a ravine looking over to the other side, the place where you ideally want to be. The biggest fear comes from the gap between the two cliffs; 'the gaping void'. The bigger the void, the greater the unknown. And the greater the unknown, the greater the fear. So if you can minimize the unknown in the void, you'll reduce the risk, and you'll feel less fear. The more you know and the more prepared you are, the safer you'll feel. And as we learnt in Day 2, if you feel safe, then you won't trigger off your *instinctive fear response* in the first place.

Napoleon Bonaparte put this rather eloquently: '*If I always appear prepared, it is because before entering an undertaking, I have meditated long and have foreseen what might occur. It is not genius which reveals to me suddenly and secretly what I should do in circumstances unexpected by others; it is thought and preparation.*'

Gulp! Wisdom

If I had six hours to chop down a tree,
I'd spend the first hour sharpening the axe.
Abraham Lincoln

Gulp! Time

Ann, a very senior human resources director in the banking and finance sector, is a strong advocate of the importance of preparation. She started her career on the fast track graduate recruitment programme in Unilever, and in her words, 'Most of the time you were thrown in the deep end and given a project you knew nothing about and asked to just get on with it.' So it was sink or swim, and she learned very quickly how to make wise decisions when under pressure. Some of her projects have involved millions of pounds and she has put her job on the line a number of times. 'I only go full steam ahead when I'm well prepared,' says Ann. 'And when I'm well prepared I'm quite happy to be brave about making big decisions. So I can take that big step and move forward.'

For Ann, preparation involves a mixture of instinct and research. First, she asks a lot of questions and does her research, asking questions of the people around her and looking at the problem from different angles. From there she forms her own gut instinct, of what feels right and what doesn't feel right. Then, once she's got a sense of the way forward, she tests out her conclusions, asking other people and gauging whether she's on the right track. And from there, she moves forward confidently. 'I always start off with research,' explains Ann. 'It's important to ask the right questions and look at the problem from different perspectives. The more you know, the more you are aware of where you could trip up, and then you can plan contingencies.' For Ann, there is always a tipping point, where she knows enough information to be confident about her way forward. She doesn't need to know all the information. 'There's a really important point where you learn to suspend your emotions and logic. Where you just learn that it is okay to not know everything. You can feel comfortable not knowing. You don't need all the answers. Just the trust in yourself that when you know "enough" you'll have the depth to get through it.'

Gulp! Wisdom

Luck favours the mind that is prepared.
Louis Pasteur

Gulp! Time

Gulp! Planning Framework

Some people hate preparation and others love it. Having some sort of framework, however detailed, really helps to cut out the clutter and focus your mind. To make it as easy as possible, I'd like to introduce you to the CIGAR coaching model as developed by Dr Anthony Grant and covered in *Solution Focused Coaching* (page 105)[3], co-authored with Jane Greene. I can absolutely vouch for the fact that this model is an excellent way of planning your Gulp!. Whenever you find yourself in a panic, simply sit down and map out the five stages. You'll gain great clarity in the process and this, of course, brings with it peace of mind.

The CIGAR model is simple and really easy to remember. So let me talk you through it and then I'll give you an example of how to apply it. You'll notice that most of the questions start with 'what'. They'll help you drill down to the essential elements that make up the heart and soul of your plan.

Here's how it works:

C. I. G. A. R. Model

- **C** — **Current Reality**
- **I** — **Ideal Outcome**
- **G** — **Gaps between C & I**
- **A** — **Action Plan**
- **R** — **Review**

Solution Focused Coaching

Current Reality

Imagine you're at the top of one cliff face. This is your current situation. Start by looking at where you are today and what is the reality of your Gulp!. Not what you'd like it to be, but what it is in reality. This means detailing both the facts of your current situation and the perception that you have about it.

Ask yourself:

- What are the details of the Gulp! I'm facing?
- What impact is it having on my life?
- What are the biggest challenges?
- What are my biggest fears?
- What *am* I confident about?
- What will happen if I don't address this Gulp! now?
- What impact will it have on other people?

Ideal Outcome

Now imagine that you've jumped over to the other cliff face which is your ideal outcome. We did loads of playing around with this in the last chapter, and now it's time to bring it all together. When you describe your ideal outcome, it's really helpful if you can paint a picture and bring it to life. Imagine yourself on the other cliff and describe what you see, what you hear and what you feel, as if you were watching a movie. Create a visual representation of your ideal outcome by creating a Vision Board, a collage of pictures that visually show your ideal.

Ask yourself:

- What outcome would I love to have in my ideal world?
- What am I doing in this ideal world?
- What am I hearing from the people around me?
- What am I feeling?
- What impact is this having on my life?
- What impact is this having on other people?

Gaps Between C & I

Now you're back on the current cliff face looking over (longingly) at the ideal cliff face. Between them lies the deep gaping void of the unknown. It feels daunting because it's so deep. But if you were able to fill some of the void up by turning the 'unknown' into the 'known', then it wouldn't be as deep or as daunting. This is the aim of this stage, to focus on plugging the gap between the current and the ideal.

Ask yourself:

- What is holding me back?
- What key areas are pivotal to achieving success?
- Which people do I need to talk to?
- What additional information do I need?
- What knowledge do I need to gain?
- What beliefs do I need to develop?
- What feelings do I need to nurture?
- Which people are crucial to my success?
- Which of all these would make the biggest difference?

Action Plan

Once you've identified the key gaps between the current cliff face and the ideal cliff face, you can start to put together your action plan; one that focuses on taking targeted action, rather than a flurry of meaningless activity. Before you prepare your action plan, spend some time centring yourself. Connect to your inner wisdom and tune into what's most important and what first steps you need to take. For each gap, prepare an action plan to plug that gap, outlining the appropriate actions, the order, the timescale, the people involved and the level of priority.

Ask yourself:

- Which actions will have the most impact?
- What do I need to practise?
- What are the first steps I need to take?
- What is the benefit of taking this action?
- Who else needs to be involved?
- What is the timescale or deadline for each action?
- What might stop me?
- What can I do if this happens?

Review

As you start to take action, you move into the void. So it's important that you build in some opportunities to reflect and review where you are and the progress you're making. And check whether you're still on track, or even if the goal posts are moving. This gives you the chance to refocus your efforts so that you are moving forward effectively. As you build bridges and move forward, it's also important to recognize your achievements and reward yourself for sticking with it.

Ask yourself:

- What progress am I making?
- What impact is this action having?
- Which new developments have popped up?
- Which refinements need to be made?
- What can I do to keep on track?
- What will I use to measure 'success'?
- What can I do to reward myself?

Gulp! Wisdom

Start by doing what's necessary, then what's possible, and suddenly you are doing the impossible.

Saint Francis of Assisi

Gulp! Time

Example: Maria Dates Again

Three years ago, Maria's husband left her for a younger woman. She was devastated and withdrew into her shell. After some challenging times and bouts of depression, she now feels ready to move on and wants to start dating again.

Gulp!

Current Reality

Maria is an attractive woman, aged thirty-five with blonde hair and a curvy figure. She works part time as a sales assistant in her local chemist. She has two children, aged thirteen and fifteen, who divide their time between her and her husband. Maria's friends (and children) have been encouraging her to get out and start dating again. But Maria feels nervous. She married young and hasn't dated many men. What's more, she's let herself go physically and her kids call her frumpy. Maria's reached the pivot point where, despite her reservations, she knows it's time to get back out there again. She misses the companionship of having a partner and now that the kids are getting older and more independent she would like to develop her own interests and hobbies.

Ideal Outcome

Maria isn't ready for a serious relationship just yet. In her ideal world she is dating a kind-hearted and honest man with a great sense of humour. They have great times together and visit different places every weekend. They are both interested in jazz and go out to clubs. Maria feels really good about herself. She has a glow about her. She feels good and looks fit and healthy. She comes across as confident in herself and attractive to her new man. She's happy, and she trusts him. Her children are much happier with their new mum.

Gaps Between C & I

Maria grouped her gaps into three key areas:

1. **Confidence.** Because she'd let herself go over the past three years she was lacking in confidence. She knew that if she worked on her appearance and improved her fitness she'd feel a lot more confident about herself.
2. **Opportunities to meet her new man.** Over the past three years, Maria's world had shrunk. She knew that if she wanted to meet someone new, she wouldn't be likely to meet him between the sofa and fridge on a Saturday night. Maria knew that she needed to create opportunities to meet her new man by getting out more.
3. **Trusting again.** Maria was devastated and disillusioned when her husband left her. She'd never dreamed he would leave her for a younger version of herself. She knew that if she was going to give her new relationship the best chance of success, she needed to let go of her past and build her trust in men again.

Action Plan

When Maria considered her gaps, she thought that improving her self-confidence was the most important one to tackle first.

Confidence Actions

1. Build her physical fitness, by taking the dog for a forty-five-minute walk, four days a week.
2. Splash out on a new hairstyle.
3. Ask her friend Beth to go shopping for some new clothes.
4. Take a pilates class once a week to build her inner strength and calm.
5. Be brave and ask her friends to tell her what her biggest strengths are.

Once she had the Confidence plan up and running, then she would start to look around at opportunities to meet new people.

Meeting New People Actions

1. Invite Beth to go with her to a jazz club in town.
2. Sign up to an on-line dating agency and just try it out.
3. Smile and greet people on her morning dog walks.
4. Catch up with friends at least once a week.

As Beth created more opportunities to meet new people, she knew that if she met a nice man she didn't want the relationship to be clouded by her baggage.

Trust Actions

1. Prepare family photo albums for her two children, and then remove all photos of her husband from the house.

2. Write down three reasons why she deserves to be loved and cherished and repeat these morning and night.
3. In her reflection time, she would imagine cutting ties to her ex-husband and consciously letting go of their past together.

Review

Maria didn't want to rush into things, so she gave herself a timeframe of six months. To check on her progress she decided to:

1. Spend a couple of hours down at Starbucks on the first day of each month checking where she is, what she's achieved and what's next.
2. Ask her friend Beth to support and encourage her.
3. Write down three goals a week on her bedroom calendar.
4. Treat herself to a luxurious bubble bath and me-time at the end of each week.

Practice Makes Perfect

Practising is a no brainer for sports people. Take a 100-metre Olympic sprinter, for example. They will spend years of training, simply to take part in a handful of ten-second races every year. Like most professional athletes, they'll spend about ninety per cent of their time training, in order to be able to perform ten per cent of the time. They focus on building their strength, their speed and their energy, as well as on embedding the skills and techniques they need to be at the top of their game. The goalkeeper will spend hours catching penalty shots to the goal. The sprinter will spend hours practising the take-off. A gymnast will spend hours practising dismounting from the bars. And the high jumper will spend hours practising the lift-off from the ground. In this way, when they're out there performing, their bodies are so attuned to what they are meant to be doing, they do it naturally and without hesitation. At top levels in sport, there can be no hesitation. A millisecond can mean the difference between the medals table and last place.

So when you look at your planning framework, what parts can you practise in advance?

For example:

- Maria could practise smiling in the mirror, or getting her new hairstyle to look like it did when she left the salon, or she could prepare her profile for the dating agency.
- Patrick can prepare himself for his job interview by practising it with his friend.
- Helena can prepare herself to stand up to her boss by practising what she needs to say in the mirror.
- Sue can prepare herself for her big presentation by practising it again and again until she knows it off by heart.
- Sara can prepare herself for her wedding by having a dress rehearsal where they practise the whole wedding ceremony.
- Allen can prepare himself for the home birth of their child by practising the prenatal techniques with his wife.
- Marielle can prepare herself to go and live in China by

taking classes in Mandarin and finding a conversation buddy.

Gulp! Reflection

Go back to your Gulp! framework and ask yourself:

- What are the most important components?
- What can I do to practise them in advance?
- What difference will it make if I practise them?

Gulp! Wisdom

Practice means to perform, over and over
again in the face of all obstacles,
some act of vision, of faith, of desire.
Practice is a means of inviting the perfection desired.
Martha Graham

Gulp! Time

Energy, Energy, Energy

As you step up and Gulp!, you'll want to be sharp and on the ball. You'll want to be able to think clearly and you'll want to stay calm under the pressure. Plus you'll want to have a full energy reservoir so that you stay alert and focused. If you can keep your energy high and vital, you'll be able to deal with anything that comes your way from a place of strength. George Bernard Shaw once wrote, '*Better keep yourself clean and bright; you are the window through which you must see the world.*' As you move through your

Gulp!, how you are 'seeing' the world significantly influences the choices you make and how you manage the ups and downs of transition and change.

Jim Loehr and Tony Schwartz have written a fantastic book called *The Power of Full Engagement*.[4] Based on sports coaching, it really opened my eyes to the whole concept of managing energy, not time. Whatever situation you're facing, while you can try and fudge looking upbeat and full of vitality, your body won't lie. It will speak in ways that you won't even realize: your eyes will say what you're really feeling deep down inside; your skin will talk about your general well-being; your voice will say a lot about how much air you've got in your lungs; the way you hold your shoulders will tell how stressed you are and that casual flicking of your hair will show people where your mind really is.

If you want to be physically prepared and in top form to face your Gulp! AND be full of vital energy that can help you deal with anything that comes your way, then you need to *minimize energy drainers* and *maximize energy gainers*. According to Loehr and Schwartz, our energy levels, at any point in time, draw from four sources of energy: *physical, emotional, mental* and *spiritual*. Take athletes, for example. Athletes spend their entire lives expanding, sustaining and renewing the energy they need to compete for focused periods of time. They build daily routines for eating and sleeping, working out and resting, mentally preparing and staying focused and connecting regularly to the goals they have set for themselves. If we want to be at our best as we step up and Gulp!, then we need to proactively manage each of these energy sources, carefully balancing energy expenditure with frequent energy renewal.

Gulp! Wisdom

Managing energy, not time,
is the fundamental currency of high performance.
Jim Loehr and Tony Schwartz

Gulp! Time

Boosting Your Energy

Water, oxygen, food, fitness and sleep are the fundamental fuels for your body. The size of your energy reservoir depends on your breathing, the foods you eat and when you eat them, the quantity and quality of your sleep, the degree to which you get 'downtime' during the day, and the level of your overall fitness. *Run low on any one of them and you'll feel the impact of the energy drain.* And if you don't have enough physical energy, you certainly won't have adequate emotional and mental energy to face your Gulp!. It will affect the way you think, the way you feel, the way you behave and the way you deal with stressful situations. What's more, when you feel fit and physically healthy, you feel more grounded and have a greater sense of vitality. This gives you that extra physical stamina you need when you're under pressure, and it will lift your mood and give you a more positive and optimistic outlook. Take Tim, for example. The day before stepping up to his big challenge he went cycling in the countryside. The weather was cool and the air was fresh. It made a huge difference to him as he faced his challenge. He had more energy, his skin had a healthy glow, his voice was stronger, he walked taller and he was able to think clearly on his feet.

Imagine stepping up to your Gulp! in peak condition, looking good and feeling great, and feeling totally energized, ready to meet whatever comes your way. Here are five simple ways to increase your physical energy and fuel your vitality.

1. Drink Well

Fifty-five to seventy-five per cent of our body weight is water, eighty-five per cent of our brain tissue is water and eighty-three percent of our blood is water. We regularly lose nearly twelve cups of water a day (I wonder how they measured that one!). That's why doctors advise that we drink two litres of water a day to replenish our system. If you drink more water your skin will have a healthier glow, your bodily functions will be operating at peak performance and you'll have much higher energy. In addition, with more water in your system you'll be fuelling your brain, leaving you more focused and clear thinking. So if you short change your body on water, you short change yourself on stamina and vitality. Here are some great ways of increasing your water intake, with little effort on your part.

1. Add lemon, lime or orange slices to your water to give it some zing.
2. Carry a half-litre bottle of water around with you and refill as needed.
3. Minimize your intake of caffeine and alcohol because they cause dehydration.
4. Get into the habit of taking a bottle of water into

every meeting, or have one by the couch while you watch TV.

5. Count the eight glasses of water and give yourself a wonderful treat at the end of the day.

2. Breathe Well

Approximately ninety per cent of the body's energy is created by oxygen. And the creation of energy from food is totally dependent on the amount of oxygen available in the cells. All the body's activities, from brain function to elimination, are regulated by oxygen. The brain alone uses twenty per cent of the body's energy and requires constant oxygen to function. Any stress causes oxygen deficiency. The best way to optimize your energy levels is to ensure that you oxygenate every cell in your body adequately. The more oxygen you have in your system, the more energy you produce. Increasing your oxygen intake is easy, and it's free. Here are some ways that you can get started immediately.

1. Walk to work or to the bus or train, and consciously take deep breaths.
2. Eat your lunch outside, or at least get fifteen minutes of fresh air during the day.
3. Spend some time in the garden, or find a park to sit in.
4. Go to the seaside and spend some time just breathing in the sea air.
5. Practise ten minutes of deep breathing at regular intervals during the day.

3. Eat Well

A critical source of energy in our lives comes from the food we eat. At the most basic level, physical energy is the result of the interaction between oxygen and glucose. When you don't renew your body with food, your energy reservoir runs low, leading to poor concentration, mood swings and lack of focus. To keep your physical energy levels up during the day it's important to sustain a steady high-octane source of energy throughout the day. There are differing opinions about diet and nutrition and it's not my aim to go into too much depth here. The key point is that to maintain steady energy levels, experts recommend that you eat at regular intervals during the day by having five to six low calorie, highly nutritious meals. So here are some top tips for you to be aware of over the next seven days:

1. Always start your day with breakfast. It replaces blood sugar depleted during sleep and kickstarts your metabolism.
2. Try to eat fresh foods rather than processed foods. They contain more natural energy.
3. Eat foods that are low on the glycemic index which slowly release sugar into the blood stream. These include whole grains, proteins, fruits like strawberries, pears, apples and grapefruit.
4. Manage your portions so that you are only eating as much as you need to drive your energy for the next two to four hours.
5. Minimize the junk food, coffee and caffeinated beverages. These produce energy 'spikes', but also prompt dehydration and fatigue in the long run.

4. Sleep Well

Other than breathing and eating, sleeping is the most important aid to recovery in our lives. It gives your body the chance to rest, repair and renew. During the deepest levels of sleep, cell division is most active, growth hormones and repair enzymes are released and muscles have the opportunity to regenerate. Although we spend thirty-three per cent of our lives asleep, we barely give it a moment's notice . . . until we *can't* sleep. For millions of people, the consequences of a poor night's sleep are higher stress, difficulty in concentrating and poorer performance. Research shows that the average person needs seven to eight hours a night, but it differs for every person. In the build-up to facing your challenge, why not take some time out and recharge yourself by getting some good nights' sleep. The quality and quantity of your sleep can make all the difference to how you feel. Here are some tips to help you sleep better:

1. Maintain a regular bedtime routine (like a soak in the bath, or listening to calming music).
2. Establish a regular wake time schedule. And give yourself plenty of time to get ready.
3. Make sure your bedroom environment is conducive to sleeping – quiet, dark.
4. Check your mattress and make sure it's comfortable.
5. Avoid caffeine (eg. coffee, tea, soft drinks, chocolate) close to bedtime as it can keep you awake.

5. Exercise Well

With all the media hype around exercise, you're probably more than aware of the key benefits of having a regular exercise programme – increased energy, faster metabolism, improved muscle tone, better health, stress reduction and higher self-esteem. Regular physical activity makes you look good and feel good. It can help build your muscular strength and your ability to better cope with the stresses of stepping up to your Gulp!. And it helps with flexibility and balance which improve your posture and the way that you physically hold yourself. One of the best things about exercise is that it can give you a feeling of accomplishment, as well as a 'natural high' every time you do it. That's because exercise stimulates the release of natural hormones called endorphins into the blood stream; chemicals produced in the brain that give you a sense of well-being. And to top it off, physical activity helps to release the build-up of stress, leaving you more relaxed as well as clear-headed.

Being active and feeling strong naturally helps your self-confidence and lifts your mood and attitude to facing your Gulp!. Regular exercise also helps you sleep better, which is important for the renewal and reenergizing of your body. Here are some ways you can use exercise to increase your physical energy and well-being. *If you have any queries or concerns check with your doctor first:*

1. Do at least thirty minutes of exercise every day for the next seven days, whether it's going to the gym, doing a class, walking, climbing the stairs, playing a game of squash.
2. Always warm up and cool down. You don't want to do yourself an injury.
3. Mix it up and vary the type of activity you do.

4. Make it fun – involve your friends.
5. Give yourself a prize for keeping it up.

Here are some ideas for bringing variety and fun into your exercise programme:

1. **Everyday Activities:** Walk to the tube, walk up the stairs.
2. **Gym Activities:** Cycling, running, swimming, aerobics, yoga, pilates.
3. **Outdoor Activities:** Walking, cycling, running, tennis.
4. **Social Activities:** Latin dancing, flamenco, ballroom dancing.

Up With Energy Gainers, Down With Energy Drainers

We've focused up to now on how you can boost your energy levels and build your energy reservoir. But there's no point in doing this if you are like a leaky bucket, with holes that leak and drain your store of energy. To maintain high energy levels you need to minimize the energy drainers and maximize the energy gainers.

We all have a certain amount of 'sludge' in our lives – niggly problems, frustrating people, unfinished tasks and clutter that slow us down and divert our attention away from the important things in life. These 'niggly' things drain our energy reservoir and reduce our sense of vitality. Every interaction with a person, a situation or an environment involves an exchange of energy. Sometimes the exchange is a negative one and your energy is drained, leaving you feeling 'flat', low in energy and like something has been sucked out of you. So avoid these! Other times the energy exchange is a positive one, your energy is boosted, and you feel fired up and 'buzzing'. So add more of these!

Gulp! Reflection

Take a moment to reflect upon what drains you and what energizes you. Then work through the following tables on Energy Drainers and Energy Gainers.

What can you do to minimize the drainers and boost the gainers over the coming days?

Energy Drainers

The people who drain me are:

____

The jobs that drain me are:

____

The times of day when I feel drained are:

____

The places that drain me are:

____

Energy Gainers

The people who energize me are:

____

The jobs that energize me are:

____

The times of day when I feel energized are:

____

The places that energize me are:

____

Balance Energy Recovery and Energy Renewal

Every minute of the day we are delicately balancing energy expenditure with energy renewal. It goes without saying that if you want to be full of energy and vitality for facing your Gulp!, then you need to have built a good energy reservoir.

Jim Loehr and Tony Schwartz, in their book *The Power of Full Engagement*, talk a lot about building 'recovery' and 'renewal' rituals into your life.

Energy Recovery Time

These are periods of time when you rest and rebuild your energy resources. They can be simple things like taking a break, napping, sleeping, putting your feet up. When you can combine this with fresh air and a glass of water, you're really giving your body a chance to replenish its energy reservoir. According to Loehr and Schwartz we should be taking a five minute break every ninety minutes. I ran a

Vitality Booster workshop for a company and they coined a phrase for this recovery period calling it a 'Vitality Break', and vowed to take it back into the workplace. Yes, taking a five minute break every ninety minutes takes time, but when you get back you'll be so much more productive – which saves time. Try it. It works.

Energy Renewal Time

Renewal times are those periods when not only do you take time out, you also do something that lifts your spirits. This is the time when you focus on your *energy gainers*. For John, this is spending fifteen minutes searching for bargains on eBay. For Sarah, this is listening to some jazz music on her iPod. For Margaret, this is meeting up with the girls for coffee. And for Pete, this is picking up the phone and surprising his girlfriend. Simple things that can really make a difference to your energy levels. When your spirits lift, your mood lifts and that influences the outlook you have.

Working out your Energy Recovery and Energy Renewal strategies will really help you move through your Gulp!. It puts you in the driver's seat for managing your own energy. It'll help you pace yourself and replenish your energy before it runs too low. As you keep your energy reservoir high, this will keep you uplifted, optimistic and positive. A powerful combination to deal with any stresses that your Gulp! might send your way.

Gulp! Reflection

Energy Recovery Time

What can you do to add recovery time to your schedule today?

Energy Renewal Time

What simple activities can you do on a daily basis to lift your spirit?

Preempt the Common Pitfalls

We've seen the power that preparation and practice can have on making our Gulp! easier and more effortless. Preparation helps the mind. It helps us become better informed so we make better choices and smarter decisions. And it makes our situation feel safer, which reduces the risk of fear throwing a spanner in the works. Practice helps the body. By going through the motions, our body becomes accustomed to what's expected and can override an instinctive response. It trains the mind in what to expect and what to instruct. It is a dynamic relationship. And we've seen how we can manage our energy reservoir, integrating strategies to keep it high and balance the energy output with the energy input.

But we're only human beings. And that means we can fall foul of the pitfalls that make us who we are. When this happens, simply stop, breathe and observe what is going on. What you are aware of, you can deal with.

Here are five common pitfalls and how to overcome them. Whatever you do, don't allow them to stop you from stepping up to your Gulp!.

1. Procrastination

You wake up with the best of intentions but never seem to get round to starting. Speak to any writer and they'll tell you about this one. The garden gets watered ten times, the kitchen and bathroom get cleaned even though you only did it yesterday and suddenly the daily newspaper becomes critical reading. There are lots of reasons why you might be procrastinating: fear of committing yourself to a particular course of action; the goal is too big; going after the wrong thing; doing what you 'should' instead of what you want, and the list goes on. The point is, as you move through your Gulp!, as soon as you become aware of procrastination:

1. Stop and observe what's going on.
2. Notice what it is you're avoiding.
3. Then take one small action (with no commitment to taking further action).
4. Stop and observe.
5. Then take another small action.

2. Over Promising and Under Delivering

This is a classic self-sabotage pitfall. We get exuberant and excited and promise a whole lot of stuff that we can't feasibly deliver, so we don't. Then we beat ourselves up about it and become despondent. This is the perfect approach to take if you'd like to reinforce your self-belief that you're never good enough or can't ever seem to do enough. John had this pattern. When he volunteered to take on a project at work to roll out a new product, he wanted to impress the boss. So he brought forward the deadlines. Of course, he shot himself in the foot and didn't deliver on time. He didn't impress his boss at all. And he felt like a failure.

If you find yourself following this pattern as you move through your Gulp!, stop and ask yourself:

1. Why you are over promising?
2. What are you trying to prove?
3. What negative beliefs are you fuelling?
4. What cycle are you repeating?

So if your Gulp! involves a promise to deliver, then just break the cycle. Don't over promise. Set a reasonable expectation and deliver magnificently.

3. Getting Sidetracked

Funnily enough, I'd just finished typing this heading when the phone rang. It was a friend wanting to know if I'd like to go for a walk. I felt like a break so we met up and we walked around the docks near where I live. On the way we stopped for a chat as we watched the kids sailing on the docks. Two hours later I found myself back where I left off. It goes to show how easy it can be to get sidetracked. Sometimes it can be hugely beneficial. You go off track and discover something new and helpful. Other times, though, it shows a lack of focus and can be an avoidance strategy, especially where time is of the essence.

If you do find yourself getting sidetracked as you move through your Gulp!, stop and ask yourself:

1. What is the benefit of going off track?
2. What am I avoiding?
3. What can I do to stay focused?

4. Feeling Overwhelmed

We are so used to being 'in control' of our lives that when change happens and we enter into the unknown it can be incredibly disconcerting. We are neither here nor there and sometimes we can't even see the light at the end of the tunnel. This can create strong feelings of panic, where everything just becomes 'too much'. There's too much change, too much going on, too much uncertainty and too many options. Some of us become paralysed and shut down. Our energy plummets and we shrink into ourselves. For others, the pressure triggers off strong emotions and tempers flare, like Anthony when he broke up with his long-term girlfriend. He became short-tempered at work and people complained to his boss. To top it off, he started making mistakes which almost cost him his job. However you react to feeling overwhelmed, it will take a toll on your health if you don't catch it and resolve it.

As you move through your Gulp!, if you feel overwhelmed at any point, simply:

1. Stop and breathe.
2. Silence your thoughts.
3. Create some space.
4. Ask yourself, 'What's the one most important thing to do now?'

5. Lack of Self-Belief

It happens all the time. You're moving onward and upward, walking tall and confidently, and then you hit an obstacle. Your confidence crumbles like a stack of cards falling around you. You feel winded and wiped out. Self-doubt kicks in. You feel uncertain. And then that inner critic pipes up and says, 'Did you *really* believe that you could make a success of it? I mean to say, you don't *really* have what it takes do you?' This is exactly what happened when Maxine decided to pursue a singing career. Everyone told her that she had such a great voice, but deep down she thought they were just being nice. So when she walked onto the stage for her first gig at the local pub and, horror of all horrors, the microphone wouldn't work, she just crumbled. She panicked. And when they did get it working again, her voice was so tight and constricted that it came out shrill and out of tune. It was her worst nightmare.

As you move through your Gulp!, if you come up against an obstacle that knocks your confidence then stop, breathe, smile and say to yourself:

1. This is a test. I *can* do this.
2. This is teaching me how to be strong. And I *am* strong enough.
3. If you're trying to put me off, then you're just going to have to think of something better than *that* to stop me in my tracks!

Gulp! Day 5 Summary: Plan & Prepare

The five things to remember:

1. You are captain of your own ship. Start each day by saying, 'I create my day.' Then chart your course and set sail.
2. Use the CIGAR model (Current, Ideal, Gaps, Actions, Review) to plan your Gulp! framework.

3. Practice makes perfect. Practise the parts that scare you the most until they become second nature.
4. Manage your energy reservoir. Maximize the energy gainers, and minimize the energy drainers.
5. Don't succumb to pitfalls like procrastination, feeling overwhelmed, or lack of focus and self-belief. Stop, breathe, observe and choose to take one small step.

Gulp! Action Plan: Plan & Prepare

The ideal outcome I choose to create is:

____

____

____

The key gaps I need to focus on are:

1. ______________________________________

2. ______________________________________

3. ______________________________________

What I need to find out is:

1. ______________________________________

2. ______________________________________

3. ______________________________________

The people I need to speak to are:

1. ____________________

2. ____________________

3. ____________________

The actions I need to take are:

1. ____________________

2. ____________________

3. ____________________

4. ____________________

5. ____________________

The one action I'm going to take TODAY is:

____

____

____

____

The ways in which I'm going to maximize my energy gainers are:

____

____

____

____

The ways in which I'm going to minimize my energy drainers are:

____

____

____

Gulp! Espresso

Start creating your ideal outcome. Work through these questions and get into action today. Do something physical to get your blood pumping and to help with any stress that might build up.

Gulp! Mediano

Spend some time today working through these questions and putting together your Gulp! framework using the CIGAR model. Start with the end in mind, and then work backwards, putting together a plan that outlines the appropriate daily or weekly goals and actions. Put together an Energy Plan, including regular exercise, breathing, good food, fun and cutting out any energy drainers. Start today. Take at least one step forward every other day.

Gulp! Grande

Start by preparing your Gulp! framework using the CIGAR model. Begin with the end in mind and work backwards. Focus particularly on the gaps and the things you don't know. Put together a plan that outlines weekly goals and actions that focus on plugging the gaps. Also, you'll need an Energy Plan, including regular exercise, breathing, good food, fun activities and cutting out any energy drainers. Start today. And take at least one step forward each day.

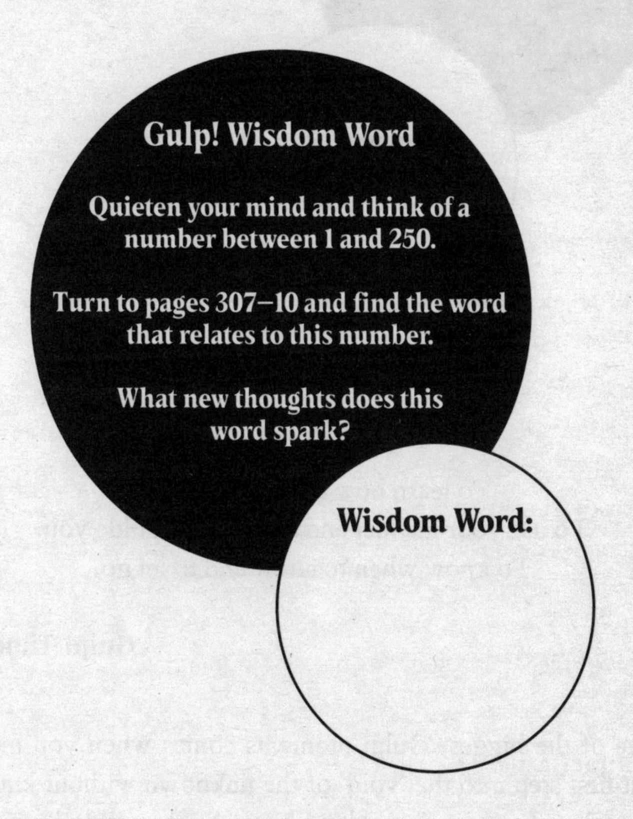

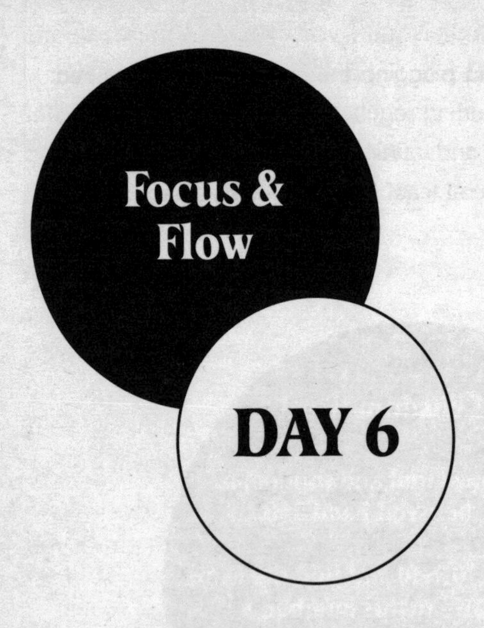

Gulp! Aims for Today

To learn how to be in the flow.
To use your instinct and intuition to guide you.
To know when to allow and to let go.

Gulp! Time

One of the biggest Gulp! moments comes when you make that first step into the 'void' of the unknown without knowing quite where you might land. It can be incredibly scary. At the same time, it can be incredibly exhilarating. The moment you step into the unknown, you open yourself up to new possibilities. You open yourself up to different stimuli and opportunities. When you are in this place and fully present and aware of everything around you, you will notice things that you didn't see before. These kickstart a chain of events that lead you to a completely new level of possibility; one that you could never have planned for or schemed even if you tried. But it does take courage.

That's why in today's session I'm going to show you how you can be more in touch and in tune with your own energy so that you can use it to guide you. We'll also talk about how you can allow and accept rather than trying to control what goes on around you. This will help you enormously to enter into the unknown, without losing your centre and balance. We'll also cover ways to sharpen your instinct and develop your awareness of coincidences, as these can provide incredibly powerful signposts to guide you forward.

And finally we'll finish off with looking at 'letting go' of anything that is still causing resistance or holding you back.

Gulp! Wisdom

What would it be like if you lived each day, each breath, as a work of art in progress?
Imagine that you are a masterpiece unfolding, every second of every day,
a work of art taking form with every breath.

Thomas Crum

Gulp! Time

Entering the Void

Gulp! Wisdom

Faith

When you walk to the edge of all the light you have
and take that first step
into the darkness of the unknown,
you must believe that one of two things will happen:

There will be something solid for you to stand upon,
Or, you will be taught how to fly.
Patrick Overton[1]

Gulp! Time

When you enter the void of the unknown you find yourself in a space where you are neither 'here' nor 'there'. Therefore, where are you? And who are you? You're back to the place of emptiness, of 'nothingness', of *wu-ji*. And as you know from Day 3, this is the space where 'the new' can emerge and be created. But it takes trust. It takes faith. It takes guts and courage to let go of 'the old' without having 'the new' already in place. But the more you can be in this gap, the more you open yourself up for powerful breakthroughs, because this is where quantum leaps can happen in your life.

This is exactly what Sarah experienced when she reached the point of 'burn-out'. A complementary therapist for over twenty years, she really enjoyed her work. Then her father died, which was actually a deeply profound experience as she was with him for the last four days and also there when he died. So although she grieved, it was not so difficult to adjust to.

But a few months later, her client numbers dropped through the floor, and she started to feel very low and exhausted. 'That's when I decided to take three months off,' recalls Sarah. 'I realized I was very close to "burn-out". So I went travelling in South America for three months.' She spent the last month in Cusco, Peru, where she explored Andean medicine, only to discover that the reason she felt so low was that she'd taken on lots of the emotional energy from her clients; hence the 'burn-out'. Feeling healed she returned home, not at all sure what she was going to do about work, since her practice was now non-existent. She was in the void of the unknown. But then events took an interesting turn. Within three weeks of returning home she had enrolled on a Masters Degree Programme to do her own research project into how clients' energy affects the practitioner, and the most effective ways for practitioners to avoid stress and burn-out. What's more she may even have the possibility of doing some supervision at the University, which could exempt her from paying tuition fees! 'What I learned from being in the void is that even though your whole world may seem to completely fall apart, as you face the challenge, exciting possibilities can open up for you in the most unexpected of ways,' says Sarah. 'I have rediscovered my passion for work again, and realize I was definitely ready for a change. But I was only able to take the leap when I was forced into it.'

Gulp! Wisdom

The unknown isn't to be feared.
The unknown is our home;
Where we all come from,
Where we are going back to.
Rumi

Gulp! Time

Being in the Flow

As you chart your course and embark on your Gulp! journey, if you travel from a place of being centred and connected to your true essence, then nature has a way of taking charge. Life starts to flow. It's as if everything is working in fine synchronization, where one thought leads naturally to another, and one action leads naturally to another. This is 'being in the flow'. Just in the same way a river naturally travels its course in search of the ocean mouth, so too do you begin to move and flow towards your natural direction. The flow can be so strong that it naturally guides you around obstacles (or over them!), finding the best path to get to where you're heading. Being in the flow creates an inertia of its own. You are propelled forward into the unknown, yet you feel less afraid. As the inertia picks up, so too does your confidence, helping you to make better choices and more rounded decisions. The inertia takes on a life of its own, inspiring you when you feel down, motivating you when you might doubt and uplifting you when things don't go quite the way you expected. When you're out of the flow, you'll know about it. Your decisions start to feel clunky and the actions you take just don't 'feel' right. When the flow of the river is blocked, the water starts to back up. Get back in with the flow and things will start moving again.

So your Gulp! journey becomes a delicate balance of *flowing forward* combined with *releasing resistance* and obstacles when they arise, or when you hit them.

Gulp! Wisdom

Flow forward.
Release resistance.

Gulp! Time

Sometimes the inertia of your flow forward can simply overcome any resistance or blocks. But more often than not, just like a river, our forward flow gets impeded when we hit a barrier. Then we have a choice; to engage a more 'forceful energy' to push through or over the barrier, or to engage a more 'allowing energy' to dissolve the block and in doing so allow the flow to begin naturally again. For me, personally, I'm more inclined to go for the 'forceful energy', which can be both invigorating and draining at the same time. But as a result of doing all the centring and connecting techniques I've become more aware of the subtle power of a more 'allowing energy'. Because I've realized that, just like a river, the natural flow can be unleashed simply by focusing on removing or dissolving any barriers or blocks. Every time I let go of something that holds me back, forward flow happens naturally. Every time I overcome a resistance, forward flow happens naturally. Every time I dissolve a block, forward flow happens naturally. And so I find myself trying less, and allowing more. The catalyst for this was doing a course in the Alexander Technique,[2] which uses minor manipulations of the body to reteach the body and mind this whole concept of 'allowing'. My teacher, Gerda Druks-Kok, has the patience of an angel. One conversation stands out:

Gerda: Point your knees towards the courtyard.
Me: You mean bend my knees?
Gerda: No Gabriella, I mean point your knees towards the courtyard.

And so I pointed my knees towards the courtyard and found my knees bending as a result.

Try this. It is such a subtle shift in focus. Bending your knees has a forceful intention, whereas pointing your knees forwards has a much more graceful and allowing effect. The point is, 'allowing' is an equally effective way to get to where you want to go. So try it out and give it a chance.

Tuning into Energy

To really optimize this approach of being in the flow, you need to be mindful of 'energy' and develop an energy calibrator. Like the water in a river, energy is the life force that flows through you and through everything around you.

Flowing Energy

This is when everything seems to fall into place and is working in sync. You feel relaxed and everything seems effortless and easy. It feels natural. Things fall into place naturally. And you just feel a sense of 'rightness' about life.

Blocked Energy

This is where you try and try, but nothing you're doing seems to be working. You can actually feel a block. Sometimes, it's because your ego is upset or attached to something and doesn't want to let go. Other times, it's because this path is simply not the right way forward for you, and you have to let go of control or your expectations. With blocked energy, step back, create space, connect to your core, breathe, expand your perspective and allow new insights to emerge.

Expanding Energy

This is when you are tapping into passion, higher creativity and greater possibilities. You feel your heart expand and your spirit lift. You feel inspired and alive. Your mood is upbeat and optimistic. You see the good in everything. Creative ideas are sparking into your mind left, right and centre. You feel expansive and may in fact be walking taller.

Contracting Energy

This is when you are trying to choose an option or a situation that doesn't serve you. Or there is something in the environment that doesn't honour and respect you or your true nature. You feel your heart sink and your spirits dive. You might even feel yourself physically shrink; your shoulders hunch and your heart sinks. Your voice becomes smaller. In fact, everything about you becomes smaller.

Bouncing Energy

This is when you seem to be bouncing all over the place. Zipping here and there with no rhyme or reason. While this can be energizing at times, if you feel yourself bouncing around too much, it's because you're not grounded. So put your feet firmly on the ground, or even stamp them down, and breathe and feel that breath going right down to your feet.

Flat Energy

This is where you are lacking in motivation and drive. Nothing seems to excite you. You feel listless, lacking in energy and you might even feel a deep sadness. This is an interesting place to be. Sometimes it's because you are in a holding pattern, at that space 'in between' one thing and another. Other times it's because you're moving away from your passion and what lights your fire. Create space to allow the new to emerge, and nurture yourself with good food, water and extra sleep to help cope with the in-between stage.

Gulp! Wisdom

Flow with whatever may happen
and let your mind be free.
Stay centred by accepting whatever you are doing.
This is the ultimate.

Zhuangzi

Gulp! Time

When Carin stepped up to her Gulp!, she experienced all of these different energies and really learned the power of being in the flow. 'Just take the first step, and then let the rest follow,' says Carin. 'Don't try and change everything at once. But take the first step, and see what unfolds next.' Carin, born and bred in Sweden, spent over twenty-seven years of her life working in the high-flying world of banking, living in Stockholm, New York, Berlin and London. Married to Fred, with two lovely sons and a successful career, Carin's life looked great on the outside. But deep inside, she was yearning for something else. 'It was when I was riding home on the bus that it would always hit me,' recalls Carin. 'No matter how great the day was, I'd always feel this deep sadness as I travelled home on the bus. I used to say to myself, "This is not what life is about!" The trouble was that while I didn't want to spend the rest of my life feeling this sadness, I didn't actually know what it was I wanted!' Then one weekend, Carin walked over hot coals at a Tony Robbins event. And that's when she reached her pivot point. 'That weekend I realized that my life could not continue as it was,' recalls Carin. 'And that's when I decided that I could no longer just think about it, I had to *do* something about it.' This was Carin's first step. And what was to unfold was a pure miracle.

She started to look at places where she could go to think and get clear on what to do next, and through her research she found the Findhorn Foundation in Forres in the North of Scotland. She decided to do one of their 'experience weeks' which involved meditation, walking in nature and self-development classes. When she spoke to her husband Fred about it, she was surprised by his response. Unbeknownst to her, Fred was also interested in going to Findhorn. So they decided to go together. 'It was just the most amazing week,' remembers Carin with a big smile. 'My main aim was to find some space to breathe and give myself the chance to see what I truly wanted in life. As soon as I arrived I felt like I'd returned to the bosom of nature. I didn't stop smiling for a whole week . . . except when I was crying! Fred and I spent precious time together doing nature walks, and also we spent time apart to get clear on our own individual thoughts.' Coming back to London was a bit of a shock for Carin, after a week of fresh Scottish air, healthy organic food and long days in nature. But the experience had given her a real sense of perspective. 'The last straw for me was getting my bonus,' says Carin. 'It was a good bonus, but that was all. I didn't feel like it justified this life that I was living. That's when I went to my boss and resigned.' Carin went home and told Fred, who was a bit shocked. But he knew that she was deeply unhappy and that she was desperate to change the life that they were living. From there, things moved very quickly. Fred took the boys to America for Easter, and Carin went back up to Findhorn for two weeks. Just before they left, they went to the bank on the spur of the moment, and got an extra mortgage on the house for £227,000. The letter of confirmation arrived just two days before Carin left for Scotland. While she was up there, she got the urge to look at houses. With a friend she drove around Forres and looked at property. 'When we came upon the house I'm sitting in now, I turned to my friend and said, "That's the house,"' laughs Carin. 'We went up to the house, which you're not supposed to do, and a lovely gentleman came to the door and said he was very interested in selling the house. So three days later I had a viewing. As soon as I stepped into the hallway I knew that this was the house that I wanted to buy. It was perfect for setting up a bed and breakfast. It was just the right feeling all over. The decoration wasn't right, but that didn't matter because it was a beautiful house with beautiful gardens.' Everything went really smoothly from there. After phone calls to Fred in America, Carin put in a closed bid for the house and it was immediately accepted. Ironically, with all the costs involved, the total sum of the house was £227,000. 'From there, things moved really quickly,' recalls Carin. 'I went back to London and we put our house on the market. The first people that viewed it made an offer which we accepted. It all took less than two months, and at no point did I feel worried, uncertain or unsure. Everything flowed just naturally. To top it off, when we finally arrived up here in Forres, it was early in the morning, and we were met with the most extraordinarily beautiful sunrise. It was amazing.'

These days, Carin and Fred are the proud owners of Villa Pilmuir, a small bed and breakfast in the heart of Forres in Northern Scotland. And in between warmly welcoming her guests and caring for her family, you'll find Carin sitting in the lounge looking out to the beautiful garden, watching the wrens play and sing in the trees. A far cry from the cold concrete and steel of London's banking district.

Looking back, Carin says, 'What's important is to take time to go inside and listen to yourself. Ask yourself questions and listen very carefully. What do you want? What is important to you? And what can you do to change this? I found that meditating really helped me get clear on what was important to me. And it wasn't to run around the City and earn City money! And be prepared for the answers that come out of the meditation,' laughs Carin. 'Sometimes it's not what you expect. And it will often mean you have to shed something; possessions, friends or even where you work or live. It can be painful. But have courage. It *is* worth it in the end.'

Gulp! Wisdom

Think of the method as a fine silvery stream,
not a raging waterfall.
Follow the stream, have faith in its course.
It will go its own way, meandering here,
trickling there.
It will find the grooves, the cracks, the crevices.
Just follow it. Never let it out of your sight.
It will take you.
Sheng-yen

Gulp! Time

Following Your Instinct

When the tsunami slammed into the coastlines of many Indian Ocean countries on 26 December 2004, it travelled over 3000 miles and left over 150,000 people dead in its wake. Caused by an earthquake measuring nine on the Richter Scale deep under the Indian Ocean, the great wave wreaked havoc, sweeping thousands of people out to sea, drowning many more and totally demolishing acres of homes and properties. Surprisingly though, very few animals died.[3] Alerted by changes in vibration and air pressure elephants fled for the hills, zoo animals retreated to their enclosures and domestic animals sought higher ground. It appears that the animals had a 'sixth sense' about the impending danger, long before the wave even hit.

When Stu was caught out in the dark of the night in war-torn Bosnia, it was his instinct that saved him and his team from certain death. Stu was an aid worker during the Bosnian war and in early 1995 he was charged with delivering a truckload of medicines to a village near Tuzla in the far north of Bosnia. The route he had to use ran along the front line at one point. He had arranged for a guide to ride with his group in the trucks to show them the way. But as fate would have it, when they arrived to pick him up, the guide was so ill he could not move from his bed. Because time was short, the guide wrote detailed instructions on a piece of paper for them. And so they set off, with Stu in the front truck navigating. Darkness was falling as they approached the front line. It was clear they were in a danger zone as they passed empty houses without roofs or windows. When Stu looked down at the notes the guide had written, his next instruction was, 'Turn right or you will be shot.' Stu swallowed nervously and as they headed through the darkness, a small road suddenly appeared leading off to the right. Before they could react, they had overshot the turning and there was another truck on their tail. It was not a good position to be in. Stu realized that turning the convoy around in the dark would be difficult and extremely dangerous. Simply going off the tarmac would increase the danger of setting off mines. But then, going on might be even worse. Stu imagined bullets shattering the windscreen, and he thought of his family back home. He didn't have long to make a decision, but he followed his instinct. He thought the side road they had passed looked too minor to be the route. It was Gulp! time for Stu. With his stomach somersaulting, he instructed the driver to move forward very, very slowly.

They inched forward gingerly. After a few nerve-racking minutes, another turning appeared on the right. They took it and made it to the delivery point safe and sound.

This is the power of instinct.

'*Instinct is the nose of the mind*,' said the legendary nineteenth-century French poet and columnist, known as Madame de Girardin. Like a mother that senses her child is gravely unwell, or a twin who instinctively 'knows' when the other is hurt, so too can we tune into a situation and get an innate 'knowing' or sense of the best idea, outcome or course of action to take. I'm sure you've experienced this in your life. You walk into a room and get the feeling that someone's had an argument. Your friend smiles and looks cheerful but you sense that she's upset about something. Someone responds to your question, but you get the feeling that they're holding back information. It's difficult to describe in words. According to the Oxford English Dictionary, 'intuition' is '*the ability to understand or know something immediately, without conscious reasoning*'. For me, it is summed up beautifully by Johann Kaspar Lavater, a Swiss theologian in the eighteenth century. He says, '*Intuition is the clear conception of the whole at once.*' It's like the final pieces of a jigsaw puzzle falling into place allowing me to 'see' the whole picture. From there I can make better judgements, better choices and better decisions.

This is what Chris felt when he saw the leaflet about the Churchill Fellowship.[4] He knew immediately that he had to apply. 'It just really stood out for me and I could feel it in my bones,' recalls Chris. Every year the Winston Churchill Memorial Trust awards approximately 100 Fellowships to enable men and women from all walks of life to acquire knowledge and experience abroad, gaining a better understanding of the lives and cultures of people overseas so they can bring this back to their communities. 'As soon as I sent off my application form, I felt really excited,' says Chris. 'I knew that it was exactly what I wanted. It felt really important to me, and that I would get through.' He was awarded an interview. It went really well and he *was* awarded a Fellowship. 'It just seemed to flow,' remembers Chris. 'One thing led naturally to the next. And in the end it just felt quite natural that I got through.'

As you step up and Gulp!, your success at navigating through that 'unknown' place between here and there will be helped enormously if you use your instinct. That means staying centred, staying connected to your true nature and following your nose. We all have this innate ability to sense and to intuit, it's just that some of us use it more than others. What's more, it must be cultivated and nurtured. The more you practise the exercises that quieten the mind to centre yourself, the more you'll find that when you are confronted with options and choices you'll sense or 'just know' the best way to turn and the best choices to make. Being able to trust yourself and your instinct in this place of the unknown is enormously beneficial. You can take steps forward towards your Gulp! trusting that you'll be able to find your way wherever you end up.

This doesn't mean you move forward in an aimless fashion. There is a subtle tension between 'focus and flow', directing and then flowing, releasing and then flowing. When you are clear on the ideal outcome, you know where you are heading. So you set the direction and chart your course. Then moving with the flow means surrendering your controlling tendencies, and being unattached to *how* you get there.

In the past ten years I've played with this a lot. It is a real art. Invariably, the *way* I get to where I'm heading is by taking a different path to the one I would have predicted. This is fun and adventurous in itself. And on the journey, other connections and link ups have arisen, making it a much richer experience.

This takes trust though. Trust in yourself. Trust in your innate wisdom. And trust in your gut feeling. Additionally, while you might have a strong sense that one path is better than the other, it takes trust again to choose the path that might not make sense to you right now, or might be the least obvious. While I have developed a strong intuitive sense, I sometimes let myself down by not listening to my inner wisdom. Instead, I choose the 'safest' bet. While I am always able to deal with the outcome, I often regret not having more faith in and trusting my instinct. It does teach me that my gut feeling holds truth and can make wiser decisions than my rational mind. As Michael Burke once said, 'Good instincts usually tell you what to do long before your head has figured it out.'

Five-Step Plan: Honing Your Instinct

As you step up and Gulp!, being able to rely on your instincts to guide you through the unknown will bring with it an incredible sense of inner confidence.

Step 1:

Connect to your centre on a daily basis to strengthen your mind, body and spiritual connection, by practising ten to twenty minutes of inner reflection every day through breathing, music, stillness, being in nature or meditation (as per the exercises in Day 3).

Step 2:

Practise 'sensing' on a regular basis by tuning into situations and seeing what 'pops' into your mind. For example, if the phone rings, sense who it might be, or when you're looking for a shop and can choose to go left or right, sense which way is the best way to go. Depending on your individual preference, images might pop into your head, or even words, or you might get a distinct feeling about something. Simply notice and observe.

Step 3:

Sense what 'expands' your energy. When you are faced with decisions, choices or options, consider each one and sense which one makes your energy expand and become light or lifts you up.

Step 4:

Sense what 'contracts' your energy. In the same way, when you are faced with a situation, choice or decision, reflect on each one and sense which one makes your energy contract and become heavy or brings you down.

Step 5:

Act on your instinct. Trust that the options, choices and decisions that expand your energy and lift your spirits are innately aligned to your true essence and true nature. Move towards these. Have the courage to follow your instinct and act accordingly. Sometimes life unfolds in mysterious ways.

Gulp! Reflection

Think about your Gulp!:

- What is your instinct telling you?
- What do you sense will work?
- What is causing your energy to expand or contract?

Noticing Coincidences

Serendipity, coincidence, synchronicity, chance – call it what you like – is an integral part of the fabric of our lives. Carl Jung[5] defined synchronicity as *'The coincidence in time of two or more causally unrelated events which have the same meaning.'*

You decide to buy a new house in a different town, and suddenly you meet someone who works in real estate from that very same town. Or you decide you want to take up salsa dancing classes, and then suddenly a flyer for a new salsa school drops through your letter box. Or you decide it's time to file for divorce and you bump into a school friend you haven't seen in years who is a divorce lawyer. For many of you, this book has landed in your lap due to a chain of coincidences, where it is exactly the right book for you to read at this time.

When you work with flow and intuition, you'll start to notice more signs of synchronicity; those chance occurrences that are like signposts that point you on your way as you step up and Gulp!. When I first started to be more conscious of synchronicity, I used to marvel at how quickly the right people, information or resources would cross my path. In fact, I used to spend so much time being amazed at the miraculous nature of the events, that I invariably wouldn't do anything with them! And so the opportunity would pass. These days I'm older and wiser. When I set out on a path, I *notice* what clues crop up on the way. In fact I *expect* synchronistic events to occur. And I consciously *attract* them to me. And I treat them as clues to help move easily and swiftly through my Gulp!.

Deepak Chopra, in his book *Synchrodestiny*,[6] writes, '*What is the meaning in a coincidence? The deeper part of you already knows, but that awareness has to be brought to the surface.*' So the coincidence doesn't necessarily dictate the action you should take. Rather it acts like a symbolic prompt. It 'speaks' to you. For example, recently I decided that I needed to get in a cleaner. I'd been mulling it over for a while, but in the same week two coincidences occurred. A flyer came through my door from a woman offering her services as a cleaner and I discovered that my neighbour's sister does cleaning locally. Both coincidences are signposts to different solutions. It's up to me now to take the meaning from them and then choose which path to take.

Coincidences are like prompts. They can trigger new thoughts, or a new awareness, that lead to the opening up of new possibilities. It's then your choice how you interpret them and what you do with them. Whether you think synchronicity is purely down to coincidence or chance, or whether you believe in the quantum nature of our world and the inherent interrelatedness and connection between all and everything, it doesn't matter. What I want you to focus on is the practical application of coincidences, how you can raise your awareness of them occurring and how you can use them as signposts to guide you.

Five-Step Plan: Attracting Coincidences

Practise attracting coincidences to you as you step up and Gulp!.

Step 1:

Connect to your centre. Use one of the inner reflection exercises from Day 3 to calm the mind and connect to your centre.

Step 2:

Make a clear intention. From this centred place, think about your Gulp! and ask yourself, 'What do I need to attract to help me move forward right now?' Set this as your intention.

Step 3:

Create a reminder. Write the intention on a Post-It note, or select a picture or object that reminds you of it. Keep this where you can see it regularly throughout the day.

Step 4:

Be observant. Over the coming days be extra vigilant and observe who or what crosses your path that could help you move forward towards your intention. When a 'coincidence' occurs, notice what thoughts pop into your mind. What does it prompt you to think of?

Step 5:

Follow your instinct. Before doing anything, reflect upon what action you feel prompted to take and sense whether your energy expands or contracts. If your energy expands and it 'feels right', take action. If your energy contracts and it doesn't feel right, incubate the coincidence and check it out again later.

Gulp! Reflection

Think about the past few days or weeks:

- What coincidences have you noticed?
- What do they mean to you?
- What could they be signalling?
- What action do you feel compelled to take?

Simple Spontaneity

Sometimes you can sit back and wait for coincidences to happen to you as you move forward on your Gulp! journey. Other times, though, you can actually consciously create the situation that allows the coincidence to occur.

In 1961, Edward Lorenz,[7] a meteorologist from MIT, was running some equations on his computer which appeared to be able to predict the weather. He came back the next day and continued running the programme from where he left off the day before. Everything appeared to follow the same sequence. But suddenly the output started to deviate in a bizarre way. He checked his equations and he checked the starting point. Both were the same. The only difference was that on the second day of the experiment he'd rounded off the fourth decimal place of the number he typed in from the previous day. By all conventional theories at the time, it still should have worked. Yet this one minute detail was enough to throw the predictions into a non-linear, seemingly chaotic direction. Under Newton's theory, a small change in the cause will result in a small change in the effect. But what Lorenz found, quite by chance, is that in a natural system like the weather, a very small change to the system applied at a certain point in time can make the future change in a very dramatic way. This discovery led Lorenz to conduct further experiments which formed the basis of what is known today as the 'chaos theory'. What they went on to reveal was that despite the completely random behaviour of the outputs, they seemed to follow a deeper order. And when they graphed the random data, the random data points started to form the shape of a double spiral much in the shape of butterfly wings.

His findings were later dubbed 'The Butterfly Effect', whereby the flapping of a single butterfly's wings in South America could have an impact six months later by causing a tornado to hit England thousands of miles away.

I hope I haven't baffled you too much with science, but here is how The Butterfly Effect can really help you on your Gulp! journey:

1. Doing that one small spontaneous action that is 'out of the norm', could shed a whole new light on your Gulp! and result in completely different opportunities opening up.
2. Just as one small change can throw things into apparent chaos, so too can one small change, or even a shift in perspective, bring immediate order into apparent randomness.
3. Trying to predict the outcomes of your actions as you Gulp! is near impossible because other things outside your control will come into play and affect them.
4. No matter how things might appear to be chaotic right

now as you face your Gulp!, trust that there is a deeper order at play here, one that is aligned to your true nature.
5. Everything that you think, feel, say and do impacts on the whole system. So what impact do *you* want to have?

Gulp! Wisdom

At the edge of unreason,
lies the underlying order of reason.

Gulp! Time

Gulp! Reflection

As you think about your Gulp!:
- When was the last time you did something spontaneous?
- What could you do to change one thing in your routine today?
- What completely spontaneous action could you take today?

Learning to Let Go

As you move in the flow, you'll start to be more aware of aspects in your life that aren't flowing. In fact they start to feel distinctly uncomfortable. What might have been a little 'niggle' in the past, has now become quite intolerable. It could be a facet of yourself and how you behave. Or it could be physical things about your home or work that are really starting to annoy you. Or it could be activities that you are doing that no longer feel 'right'. And it could also be other people, how they are behaving and how they treat you. This is an inherent consequence of change. As you start to move towards the new, you'll start to see your current situation with new eyes, and see things around you in a different light. What might have been acceptable in the past becomes no longer acceptable, because it cannot support the new person that you're becoming. That's why it'll feel uncomfortable.

The truth is that we resist change and hang on to 'the old' for as long as we can. That's because we are *attached* to it. It is our identity. It defines us and who we are. It is our world. It is our safety zone. It's what we know. And it's what we're familiar with. No wonder we're attached to it! But stepping up to your Gulp! will mean moving from 'the old' and into 'the new'. And to embrace the new, you need to let go of the attachments you have to the old. You need to let go of the things that hold you back and no longer serve you or bring out the best in you. This in itself creates a mini Gulp!. It takes incredible trust and self-belief to let go of something that has been important to you, before the new has arrived. There is always that 'no man's land', where you're neither here nor there.

Gulp! Wisdom

Just as a bird cannot fly if it has stones tied to its leg,
So we cannot make progress on the spiritual path,
If we are tied down by the chain of attachment.
Geshe Kelsang Gyatso

Gulp! Time

The power of attachment is beautifully expressed in this wonderful quote by Geshe Kelsang Gyatso,[8] a renowned Buddhist teacher. What we are attached to holds us back. When we can let go of our attachments, whether it's to a particular outcome, or a person, or a belief, we stop trying to control things and create the space for something different to happen. Something spontaneous. And something possibly even better than we imagined.

Personally, I find this one of the hardest parts of the Gulp! journey. I tend to hold on to the old well past its use-by date. I try to fly with stones tied to my legs. It slows me down. It hinders my progress. It stops me from flying to the heights of my true potential. And it's blooming sweaty hard work!

But luckily I had an epiphany once, that really helped me to get clear on the reasons why. In my garden I have a border of beautiful roses. Every summer they come out in full bloom and delight the neighbours as they walk past them on their way to work. My neighbour Jean, who is the fount of all knowledge when it comes to gardening, explained to me that if I pruned the roses down to about a foot high at the end of autumn, they would grow bigger and fuller the following summer. So as autumn came to a close, I got out there with my pruning clippers and started to cut each rose bush down to about a foot high. It felt drastic. It felt very severe. And it felt cruel. In fact the first time around, I cut them down to about a foot and a half high. I couldn't bring myself to clip them right back. True to her word, the roses did bloom thicker and pinker the following summer. And each year, the more I cut them back, the more abundant they grow.

Pruning the roses has made me realize that sometimes you

can be putting time, energy and effort into aspects of your life that are no longer right for you, that no longer serve where you're heading. When you cut them back, or let them go, you stop wasting your precious sap and energy supporting what no longer works for you. And quite simply, that means your energy can then flow into growing what *is* right for you.

Now whenever I get out there with my pruning clippers, it becomes quite a cleansing experience. With every branch I trim down I ask myself, 'What do I need to let go of from my life right now?' And then with the next branch, I ask myself, 'What else do I need to let go of?' Needless to say, it produces some very enlightening thoughts.

The difficult part of letting go is the sense of loss that comes with it. We become very attached to things; to people, to possessions and even to expectations, beliefs and attitudes. So much so, that we identify with them. We are holding on tightly to them. We don't want to 'lose' our job, our money, our partner, our reputation, our respect, our status. So when we let them go, it's like we are losing a part of ourselves. Whatever you need to let go of, the more important it has been in your life the deeper is the sense of loss. And loss can be painful. It can really hurt. It can really wrench your heart.

But until you let go, you'll struggle to move on.

When Elaine tried for a baby and failed, it really highlighted how attached she was to her beliefs and expectations. Learning to let go was her big lesson. 'Once we'd made the decision to try for a baby, I expected to go home that night and be pregnant the next day,' recalls Elaine. She and Clive were in their late thirties, had been married for some time and both had successful careers in banking. 'We made the decision one night when we were out with friends who had just had a baby girl, and because I've always had high expectations of achieving I thought we'd be successful straight away.'

But they weren't. After much trying, day after day, month after month, Elaine still wasn't pregnant. The months turned into years, and finally after two years of disappointment, they went to see a doctor. 'I felt like a real failure,' remembers Elaine. 'I'm used to driving and getting results and I realized I wasn't getting anywhere with this one. What's more there was this expectation that I'm a woman, I'm supposed to be able to do this. And then, of course, there was that sinking feeling that maybe we'd left it too late and now I was going to have problems.'

Clive agrees, 'In the back of my mind, I often thought that it might be me. So I put myself through the complete embarrassment of having some tests done. It was so embarrassing.' Clive laughs. Elaine too had further blood tests and a scan, and they confirmed that everything was fine.

Then they decided to try a course of non-interventional egg enhancing treatment for six months. 'I took my tablets every day,' says Elaine. 'But I remember the first month being absolutely devastated because I thought this would work. And it didn't. I just bawled my eyes out.'

Clive and Elaine kept with it. 'We tried . . . er . . . everything. And sometimes we were genuinely so tired. But we kept going.'

But still no luck.

Then, with only one month left to go of the six-month treatment they were at the point of giving up. There seemed to be little hope now. They were both so disappointed.

Then a miracle happened. Later that month, Elaine missed her period. And two weeks later, the good news was confirmed when she did a pregnancy test and found out that finally, after all these years, she was pregnant.

'We were amazed. It was unbelievable,' says Elaine. 'It was my last cycle of the treatment and it was so weird that that was the month it happened. Then, when we saw the scan a month later and saw the baby's image instantly, we were walking on air. We were so happy.'

Gulp! Wisdom

Release
Let Go
Allow
Flow

Gulp! Time

Gulp! Reflection

Silence your thoughts, centre yourself, breathe deeply and spend some time observing your Gulp! situation.

- What are you attached to?
- And what do you need to let go of?

	Attachment	Let Go
Beliefs:		
Expectations:		
Emotions:		
Relationships:		
Possessions:		
Ego:		

Alchemizing Fear in the Moment

There's nothing like being in the void of the unknown, going with the flow and then hitting your head against a hard obstacle; one that sparks your fear and brings you to a halt. No matter how well prepared you are and how much you're in the flow, it's likely that in the heat of these moments fear will flare up. As we've seen, it's instinctive and happens before you even know it.

It would be such a shame to get cold feet at this point!

I know it's easy to sit here with the book on your lap and rationalize your fears as you read. For some of you, the simple act of working through The Challenge Cycle will dispel many of your fears. For others, who are biting the bullet on something big for them, all the rationalizing in the world may not make a huge difference when you're in the Gulp! moment and your *instinctive fear response* takes over.

Whatever your situation as you flow forward, if you are aware of your *instinctive fear response* you're able to catch your fears in the moment. Then you can literally stop, breathe, observe the fear. As soon as you're able to observe your fear, then you're not 'in' it and acting reactively. When you are aware of your fear then you can take steps to transform the adrenaline and energy that will naturally ensue into something that motivates you rather than hinders you.

To stay in the flow, what I'd like is for you to be able to catch your instinctive reaction in the moment and to 'create space' before responding. Then I'd like you to feel confident that you can 'alchemize' your fear in the heat of the moment, transforming it from something that halts your flow and holds you back, into a force that propels you forward.

'Alchemy' is an ancient and esoteric art, almost as old as civilization itself. Although the origins of alchemy[9] are unclear, it was first practised over 2000 years ago in ancient China and Egypt, before finding its way to Greece, Rome and the rest of Europe. Alchemists sought to transform base metals (e.g. lead) into silver and gold, using a mystical process working with science, nature and philosophy. The art of alchemy is regarded as the foundation of chemistry as we know it today. The basic process of alchemy is often summed up with the Latin words *solve et coagula* which means 'dissolve and combine'.

Gulp! Wisdom

Beneath every fear
Lies the pearl of hope.

Gulp! Time

Beneath every fear lies a pearl. Focus on the fear and you'll never be able to see what lies beneath it. Release the fear, and you'll see the pearl. By taking the alchemist's approach to fear, we can stop wasting energy on denying fear, trying to quell it or trying to conquer it. Instead, we can focus our time on transmuting it from a negative and potentially debilitating energy, into a positive energy, one with momentum and a driving force.

Here is a simple process that you can use any time, anywhere for any situation. It works on transforming the energy of fear, and can be done in minutes (or even seconds) and draws on some of the principles I learned from Silvia

Hartmann's energy healing techniques.[10] It's especially powerful for your Gulp!, because it will help you neutralize fear in the moment that it happens. I'd love you to try this out and practise it again and again. I'd love for you to feel absolutely confident as you move through your Gulp!, knowing that you have a strategy for alchemizing fear the instant it arises. Imagine being able to cope with fear in the moment and neutralize it. What impact would that have on how you approach your challenge in the first place?

Alchemizing Fear

Face it
Examine it
Alchemize it
Reshape it

Gulp! Time

F = Face It

Face your fear. In *Conversations With God*, Neale Donald Walsch writes that, '*what you resist, persists*'. That's because by the very nature of resisting something you are giving it energy. In trying not to think about something, you are actually using energy in thinking about *not* thinking about it. The more energy you give it, the more energy you will need to use to resist it. And that's how fear conquers you. Instead, when you cut right through it, when you name it and come face to face with it, it can no longer hold any energy. That's because you make it 'real'. When it's real, you can deal with it.

Stop, centre yourself, breathe and then ask yourself:

- What am I afraid of here?
- What am I most afraid of?

E = Examine It

Examine your fear. What was it about the situation that triggered the fear? Was it a person, a tone of voice, a sound, a smell or a place? As we've seen with the brain, most of our fears are based on past experiences. Does this trigger hold true now, in this different time, different place and different situation? Remember you are also different. So break it down and observe it for what it is. Then you can decide whether your *instinctive fear response* is actually still appropriate. Is this a life or death situation? Or can you neutralize this fear because it's no longer relevant.

Ask yourself:

- What's the trigger here?
- How does this situation remind me of a past experience?

A = Alchemize It

Alchemize your fear. It's time to clear it. Let it go. Allow it to dissipate. The simple act of doing this will release any hold it has on you. To alchemize your fear, locate where you feel it in your body. Is it in your stomach? Your heart? Your throat? Now inhale deeply. As you breathe out, imagine releasing the fear with your out breath, dissolving it into the air around you. You can do this through pure intention, or you can use more visual techniques, like physically blowing it out and away. Keep doing this and as you breathe out your fear, you'll notice that it becomes less prominent.

In addition, as you breathe out your fear say to yourself:

- I dissolve this fear from my memory and my mind. And I do it now!
- I release this fear from every cell in my body. And I do it now!
- I let go of this fear from my past, present and future. And I do it now!

R = Reshape It

Reshape fear into hope. As you alchemize your fear by breathing it out you'll notice that you start to feel more 'neutral' about your situation. The last stage of the alchemy process is reshaping and unifying everything back into a state of wholeness, harmony and balance. This is where hope comes in. Hope brings a higher, more positive energy that can help 'pull' you through the experience. This time, I want you to imagine that you are surrounded by the energy of hope. It's bright, light and vibrant. Now simply breathe in hope and feel it being transported to every cell in your body. You can simply use intention, or you can imagine breathing in a beautiful coloured mist or light. Just keep breathing in hope, and feel yourself expanding and becoming lighter.

You can add to this by imagining:

- What is the best thing that could happen?
- What are all the great things that could come out of this?

You *can* move through this challenge. So let hope be your friend. Let the pearl of hope lift you up out of fear, and into an exciting place of possibility and opportunity.

Gulp! Recap

So remember, even in the heat of the moment you can *alchemize fear.*

Face it. Name the fear.
Examine it. Find the trigger of the fear.
Alchemize it. Breathe out the fear.
Reshape it. Breathe in hope.

Gulp! Time

Gulp! Day 6 Summary: Focus & Flow

The five things to remember:

1. Be the creator of your life. Chart your course and then flow with it.
2. Let your intuition and instinct guide you.
3. Watch out for the signposts of coincidences and synchronicity.
4. Learn to let go and allow. It frees you to flow forward naturally.
5. Alchemize fear in the moment. Breathe out fear. Breathe in hope.

Gulp! Action Plan: Focus & Flow

My instinct is telling me that:

____

____

____

The coincidences that I've noticed are:

1. ______________________________

2. ______________________________

3. ______________________________

The things I need to let go of are:

1. ______________________________

2. ______________________________

3. ______________________________

What I want to attract into my life right now is:

1. ______________________________

2. ______________________________

3. ______________________________

The spontaneous action I'm going to take is:

____

____

____

____

Gulp! Espresso

Centre yourself and simply tune in to what you want to create. Use your intuition to guide you today. If you feel fear, alchemize it in the moment.

Gulp! Mediano

In your centring session, focus on what you want to create. Then every time you notice a coincidence, write it down in your journal, and write down the significance and meaning that it holds for you. Sharpen your intuition by listening to it on a daily basis and using it to guide you. Start to let go of things that are holding you back, and if you feel fear, alchemize it in the moment.

Gulp! Grande

At the end of each centring session, tune in to what you want to create and wait for your intuition to speak about the next actions to take. When you notice coincidences, write about them in your journal and take the action that feels right. Play with your energy meter; notice when your energy expands, when it contracts and when it feels flat. Do one spontaneous thing every day. And focus over the next few weeks on letting go of everything that is holding you back. Let your intuition guide you.

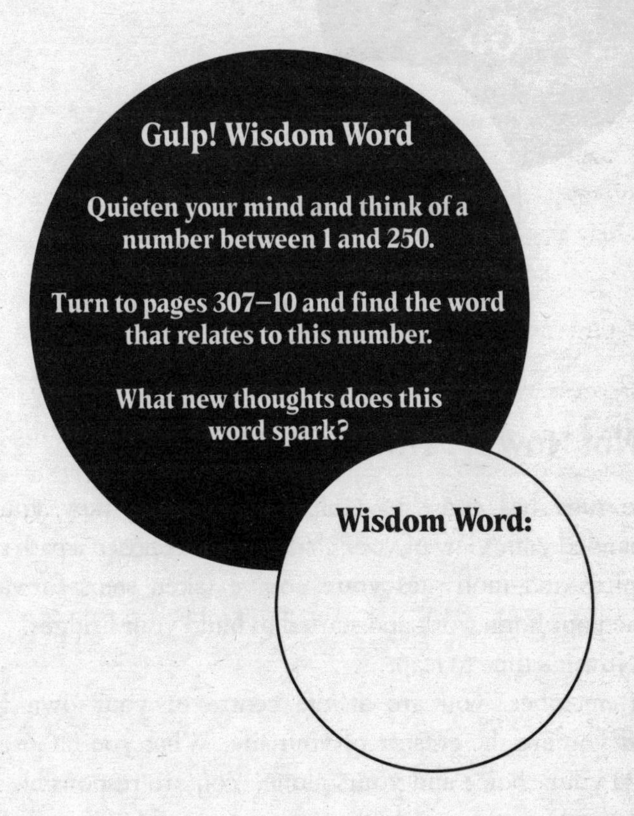

If Not Now . . . When?

The time has come to Gulp! and Go. By now you've expanded your view of your challenge and chosen a path that inspires and motivates you. You've taken steps forward, done your homework and started to build your bridges.

Now it's time to leap.

Remember, you are at the centre of your own life. And you are the creator of your life. What you choose to do is your choice and yours alone. You are responsible for making those choices. And you are responsible for accepting the consequences that come out as a result. Embrace this responsibility. Truly be the creator *of* your life, and creator *in* your life.

Gulp! Wisdom

'Come to the edge,' he said.
They said, 'We are afraid.'
'Come to the edge,' he said.
They came.
He pushed them . . .
And they flew.
Peter McWilliams

Gulp! Time

As we near the end of our journey together I want to give you one last boost to make this final leap and tie up any loose ends. This will help you stay calm and centred in the moment, and help you deal with anything that might potentially throw you off course. Mark this page. And if you ever feel lost or confused at any point on this Gulp! journey or any future ones, then simply stop, come back to this page, breathe and read.

Because here are seven signposts to give you a boost and direction:

1. Dare yourself to step up to it and defy anything that holds you back

Name the challenge and face it head on. This is an opportunity for you to learn and grow. This is your chance to create an important breakthrough in your life. This is your option to let go of those things that hold you back. This is your time to say 'no' to any more pain, frustration and suffering, and say 'yes' to a life where you feel vibrant and fully alive. This is the time to live your true life. You've reached a pivot point. Embrace this opportunity with both arms. And trust that you'll get through it.

Key Words: Name the challenge. Embrace it. Trust.

2. Break down your worries and anxieties and break through your fear

It's natural to feel afraid because you're stepping outside your comfort zone and into the void of the unknown. The bigger the Gulp!, the greater the fear. But don't blame the situation for your fear. Blame your mind. You created this fear. Your mind triggered it based on your thoughts, your beliefs and your interpretations. So use your mind to reverse it. Separate the reality of the situation from your perception of the situation. Then look for the positive. Focus on the benefits. Command your mind to do so. When you change your perception to a positive one, your feelings of fear will dissolve.

Key Words: See the reality. Notice your perception. Master your mind. Concentrate on the positive.

3. Connect to your core and build a strong centre

When you quieten your mind, you silence the very thoughts that create fear and worry in the first place, so you can disarm them completely. When you connect to your core, you find *wu-ji*, that inner place of stillness where there are no thoughts, no fears, no judgements and no worries. Here there is no ego, only your true essence. Here is your inner strength and personal power. Here is your higher wisdom. And above all, here is the space from where 'the new' can emerge and be created. So create space today to spend time in stillness, silence and deep reflection. Practise silencing your thoughts and managing the chit chat in your mind by simply commanding it to stop. Breathe deeply and fully. Consciously be in the present. Connect to nature and the power of music.

Action: Stop. Get fresh air. Breathe. Silence your thoughts.

4. Imagine new opportunities and invent new possibilities

When you find inner calm you can hear your higher wisdom. This is a powerful space for creation. What you create from this place is pure and aligned to your true nature. So don't settle for the first solution you think of. Use this opportunity as a catalyst to really make some lasting and transformational changes to your life. Open your mind. Stretch it. Expand it. Spark your imagination. Extend your perception of what could be possible. Be brave and challenge the status quo. Don't think of 'what is', ask yourself 'what could be?' You are the creator of your own life. So what do you want to create? Imagine, dream and allow magic to happen.

Key Words: Spark. Expand. Imagine. Dream.

5. Prepare yourself and practise, practise, practise

Choose the path that inspires and motivates you. Hold the bigger vision and start moving forward. Being in the void is always an unknown quantity. Yes, you can make the leap blindly. Or you can reduce the risk by plugging the gaps and building footbridges. As you move towards your Gulp!, determine what you know, and what you don't know. Use your centring techniques to tune into what's really important and to guide you towards exactly the right people, places and information you need. Put a plan in place; not a rigid plan but a loose framework that you can flow with. Then start building footbridges. Practise what you need to say. Practise the big moment itself. Practise keeping cool, calm and collected. The more you practise, the less challenging it will feel. Build your physical energy reservoir and minimize energy drainers, so that when you step up you are in top form.

Key Words: Chart your course. Plan. Prepare. Practise. Build Energy.

6. *Focus on your chosen path and go with the flow*

As you move forward towards your big Gulp!, *don't* try and control every outcome. Instead, remain calm and centred in the void of the unknown and use your intuition and instinct to guide you. Look out for coincidences or examples of synchronicity that act as signposts. In fact, consciously attract them to you. When you're faced with a decision or choice, use your energy calibrator to guide you; if your energy expands, move forward; if your energy contracts, stop and question. And decide what you need to let go of because it's holding you back from truly being in the flow. And stay centred and in the flow. Each foot forward feels easy and graceful. It feels 'right'. Remember, you are the creator of your life in any moment.

Key Words: Focus. Flow. Release. Flow. Signposts. Flow. Let go. Flow.

7. Just Gulp! and go for it

You've done everything you can to make this Gulp! a success. You've calmed your mind, mastered your fear and you see your challenge from the place of possibility. You're moving forward in the flow and you've prepared yourself and practised. No more waiting. No more preparing. *You are ready*. It is Gulp! time. So take the leap of faith. Know that it will be graceful and swift. And know that when you land on the other side it will be with both feet on the ground, balanced and poised.

Key Words: You are ready. It's Gulp! time. Move swiftly and gracefully.

Leaving a Trail

Gulp! Wisdom

Do not go where the path may lead,
go instead where there is no path and leave a trail.
Ralph Waldo Emerson

Gulp! Time

I love this quote from Ralph Waldo Emerson, the American nineteenth-century poet. It could be something to do with being the offspring of pioneering folk, and it's probably got a lot to do with my passion for innovation and creativity.

Being the creator of your life means taking responsibility for it, and for the choices you make.

In your Gulp! journey, many choices you make will be

challenging and changing the fundamental beliefs that you hold true about yourself. That's because you cut through the conditionings of your thinking and dial straight in to your true nature. What you perhaps don't realize, is the ripple effect this has on the people around you. Your loved ones, friends, family and colleagues will see what you're doing. They might resist your changes at first. They love and care about you, and may not want to lose the 'old you'. Because when you change, they have to as well, because you've shifted the dynamics between you. But they too will start to question their own life. It will get them thinking. They may start to look outside the box and open their eyes to realize what could be possible in their own lives. It might even completely change their views on the world. And it might even provide them with the impetus to make their own Gulp!

So know that every time you Gulp!, you shine the light for the people around you, even though at the time you might not realize this. You become a catalyst for change and an inspiration for others. You become a trailblazer.

And if you ever need a small reminder in the heat of the moment, just visualize these three steps:

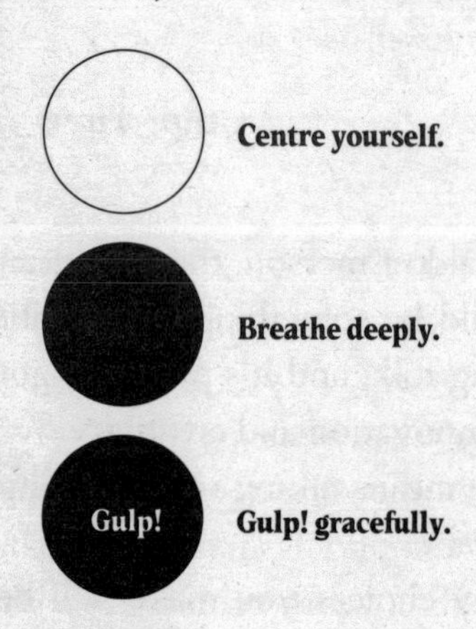

Before I go, let me leave you with three inspirational stories from people who have faced a big Gulp! in their lives.

Once you've read them, sit and reflect for a moment. Then ask yourself . . .

If not now . . . when?

Gulp! Wisdom

The breeze at dawn has secrets to tell you;
Don't go back to sleep.
You must ask for what you really want;
Don't go back to sleep.
People are going back and forth across the doorsill
where the two worlds touch.
The door is round and open.
Don't go back to sleep.
Rumi

Gulp! Time

The Brewing Gulp!

Linda's Story

'After working so hard for four years to get my business off the ground and then having to give it all up and let it go, *that* was what made walking the Camino[1] seem possible,' says Linda, social entrepreneur and mother of three sons, as she remembers her epic journey. 'El Camino' is an old Christian pilgrimage route that started in the twelfth century, to visit the bones and burial place of Saint James. But it is no short walk in the park. Running from Saint Jean Pied de Port in the French Pyrenees, the mountainous route cuts across the north of Spain, finishing 500 miles later at the Cathedral in Santiago de Compostela. Marked with bright yellow arrows, most people take at least a month, hiking about fifteen to twenty miles a day over rugged mountains, through valleys and stopping overnight at basic *refugios* that dot the route.

Linda first heard about the Camino when she visited a relative in Spain. They were doing a tour of the Cathedral in Santiago, and the guide was talking about the pilgrims who came from all around the world to walk the Camino. For Linda, it touched something deep inside her as she thought of how brave the pilgrims were to do the 500-mile journey, alone and isolated.

But then life took over and she forgot about it. That was, until a few years later, when she was faced with one of the biggest challenges of her life. Due to unfortunate circumstances, she was going to have to give up the business that she had built from the ground up and nurtured and reared. 'It was a really tough decision,' recalls Linda. 'I was going to lose my business, lose my steady income and lose my beautiful home. All these things that were so dear to me. I knew that to cope with it all I had to find a way to help me get through it. And I knew it was going to have to be something quite big and radical. I knew that I had to do it alone, and I knew that I had to let go of all the material things that I'd acquired over the past few years. I knew I was going to have to let all that go and get back to basic bare bones.'

Then, at one of her lowest moments, Linda was sitting in front of the computer at the office and she had a spark.

Something prompted her to remember the pilgrims and El Camino. 'As soon as I had that spark, my mind was made up and there was no going back,' remembers Linda. 'I knew that the Camino would help me with letting go. Some people say that the Camino is a call, that you don't choose it, that it calls you.'

Coincidentally, a few days afterwards Linda took on a new client. She had cycled to Santiago the year before, and could point her in the direction of books and websites that could help her plan the trip. So this sealed it for Linda, and she decided to go.

Once the decision was made, she felt a sense of bubbling excitement. 'At least I knew then that my life wasn't going to come to an end when I left the business. I had somewhere to go and something to do,' says Linda. 'But I was petrified as well. In fact my mind wouldn't allow me to think about the isolation and loneliness. And obviously my sons weren't overly happy. They wanted me to have a nice cosy cruise!'

Linda spent the next few months preparing for her journey at the same time as winding down the business. Her priority was to do it in the safest way possible. 'I'm seriously not the outdoorsy type,' says Linda. 'And I was a woman, walking it alone, so it was quite risky. And of course, without being dramatic, you do have to come to terms with all sorts of outcomes. I had to come to terms with the fact that something could happen. Mentally, you do have to get to the place of knowing that.'

She bought some great books and they really helped. She trusted that everything she was doing was right, that the timing was right and that the thinking was right. That became her theme, to look out for sparks of synchronicity.

So she started to make the journey interesting before she even went. She bought an MP3 player and loaded all her favourite upbeat tracks to keep her going. Of course, she did a lot of fitness training, walking in the local conservation area with her rucksack on her back. Three times a week she went walking up and down hills. She attracted a few odd stares. People thought she was a bit mad, walking in the gardens with her big backpack on.

Then the big day came. It was 18 May, her day of departure. Armed with her small rucksack (less than ten per cent of her body weight) packed with the bare basics, she left for Saint Jean Pied de Port. Originally, she thought she'd arrive at Saint Jean Pied de Port and then get the train around the Pyrenees to Roncesvalles. That way she wouldn't have to do the gruelling walk over the Pyrenees. But when she got to Biarritz airport, she immediately met other pilgrims who were heading off from Saint Jean Pied de Port. Feeling a bit wimpish about missing out the Pyrenees, Linda got on the train to Saint Jean with everyone else, and teamed up with an Irish woman.

'The first day was absolutely gruelling for both of us,' recalls Linda. 'I really didn't know whether I was going to be able to make it. It was just such a huge shock to the body. It was so hot and we did very little walking. Then on the second day I went off alone and the Irish woman slept in, and I ventured up the Pyrenees all by myself. That was the turning point for me! It was incredibly steep, and there was melting snow. When I got to the top, I was just so elated that I had done it. And there was a Madonna statue at the very peak, a monument, and I left my starfish badge there, my memento of my business. So that was powerful closure for me.'

Surprisingly, despite not being the outdoorsy type, Linda was one of the first of their group to arrive at Roncesvalles. She felt really chuffed. The next day she got up early and was feeling positive and competent. She could do this! Then she fell down a ditch. 'I injured my knee quite badly,' remembers Linda. 'And that changed everything for the rest of my trip. Literally, I was never in a strong position again. My knee became extra baggage to carry. It swelled up and I had to take a taxi to a medical centre. I couldn't walk very fast. So everyone in the original group left, and went ahead. I found myself back on my own, with no contacts, a knee that was difficult to walk on and just feeling incredibly isolated. That was one of the toughest times. It would have been really easy to say, "I've injured my knee, let's go home." But I couldn't do that. I just could not face coming back home and accepting I'd given up the business. Walking with a bad knee by myself was a better outcome for me. That's how bad I was feeling at that time; I couldn't face the truth of the business.'

So she kept walking, learning to deal with pain in a way that she had never dealt with it before. That got her very focused on survival. 'You're out there, just you and your rucksack and the occasional bar on the way. Sometimes other pilgrims pass you. But I didn't speak French or Spanish, so it was difficult to ask for help. And anyway, they were getting on with their own walk. It really focused me on survival which is great training, because it forces you to be in the moment. And that was one of the biggest gifts, to learn to live in the moment. You see so much more. You see the beauty of the most simple things. Funnily enough, if I was fitter, I would have been more focused on how fast I could walk today. But because I injured my knee, that was never an option for me. So it forced me to focus on the walking and completely being with myself.'

And so she kept walking. At night she stayed at albergues and refugios along the way, basic hostels with bunk beds all clamped together, basic showers and toilets. There was no food, and you had to find a bar to eat at in the evening.

'Mostly I preferred walking on my own,' says Linda. 'But now and then I walked with other people. The thing with other people, particularly when your knee isn't brilliant, is that you find yourself speeding up to keep up with them. When you speed up, you lose your walking rhythm and the walking becomes so much harder. Even talking and walking becomes hard in itself. But when you walk on your own, you find a natural rhythm with yourself. You bring into balance your walking and your thinking, and you can push yourself through really tough barriers a lot more easily.' There were some fun times as well. Linda recalls the time she walked with a lovely, albeit slightly nutty, French lady. And there was a Belgian couple who were great fun. But most of the time she chose to walk on her own and meet up with people in the evening at the hostels. Sometimes it would be new people, and other times it would be people she'd met a few weeks before and was reconnecting with.

And so the days passed. Each day started out between 5.30 and 6am, walking about eight hours through the rough terrain to arrive at the next hostel by 2 or 3pm when the sun became too hot to walk.

But when she had about twenty kilometres to go, things took a turn for the worse. 'I'd had a nasty experience with a guy at a hostel,' recalls Linda. 'It really upset me and I felt homesick and a long way from my family. If I wasn't so tired and depleted maybe it wouldn't have been so bad. But I got really upset. I befriended him as a co-pilgrim and he crossed the line, reminding me that you can't always be sure of someone's motives. And so it really upset me. Two American women took me under their wing and we went to stay at a hotel. The next day, they decided to get a taxi the rest of the way. They were both in their sixties and were exhausted, and one of them was recovering from a chest infection. They asked me to join them. But I said no. No, I've got to finish this myself. So they went off and I carried on walking. And that day I fell and twisted my ankle, the opposite one to my knee. And that was mostly due to tiredness. I wasn't walking well and I was just dragging my feet. It was really painful. My ankle swelled up and I finished my walk early that day and went to a bar to have something to eat. Then I got stung by a bee – the same bee – twice! It had been on my wine glass and it stung my palm. And as I shook my hand it landed up on my finger and stung that. So my palm was throbbing, my finger was throbbing and my ankle was throbbing. The next day I got up and I was probably just over one day away from Santiago. It would have meant another night in a hostel. My ankle was really swollen. Ironically, my knee wasn't feeling too bad by comparison. It was six in the morning and I was walking along with a throbbing ankle and hand, and I thought to myself, "What on earth am I doing? Would Saint James really want me to do this?" And at that instant I remembered my friend Rick who has this concept that it's "all made up". It got me thinking. What if this whole Camino spiritual pilgrimage thing was all made up and Saint James was up there looking at us struggling, laughing his head off.

'That day, I had one of the best conversations with myself, about how I do this, how I push and push myself and stay much longer than I should, even when the journey's over. It was the same with the business. I stayed with it a lot longer than I should have. Because I didn't want to sell. I didn't want to let people down. I wanted to be seen to be doing the right thing. And here I was on the Camino, so damaged and tired, and yet I was still struggling well past the call of duty. And it was a complete mirror of what I was going through with the business. That was the moment that everything fell into place. It was all so simple. So I thought I'd get a taxi the rest of the way. But where was I going to find a taxi in the middle of the Camino? I waited until I reached the next village with a bar. But when I got to the bar, I was too embarrassed. It was crowded with pilgrims getting ready to go to Santiago. And I was too embarrassed to ask them to call a taxi to come to the bar and get me, even though I looked a real mess. So I got back on the road and started walking again. Then I saw this tiny little sign that directed me to another bar. It was totally off the track. As I was walking towards it, I could see the bar, and I was thinking to myself, "Am I going to ask for coffee or am I going to ask for a taxi?" Anyway, I got in there and I just said, "Can you get me a taxi?" Then I sat down at the table and cried and cried. I can't tell you how much I cried. It upsets me so much thinking about it. I think I just cried because I was just so relieved that it was all over. It was so emotional. Then the taxi came and I limped over to it. The taxi driver was so sympathetic and I just sat down in a lump. I was so relieved. Finally it was over.'

The taxi driver took her directly to the main square in Santiago. As she got out of the taxi she joined a group of pilgrims with some musical instruments. It was 18 June, exactly a month after she had started her epic journey. 'And so it looked like I'd just arrived with this group of people,' continues Linda. 'But honestly the day turned out to be one of my best days. And I'm sure it was Saint James saying, "That's what you needed to know." I went through the registration and wrote down how far I'd come. And when I looked at the register, I was surprised; not only was I the only person from the UK, but I was the person that day who had come the furthest. Nobody else had come from Saint Jean de Pied de Port. At that moment, I realized how brave I'd been and how well I'd done. Okay, I got a taxi for the last twenty kilometres, but I'd done amazingly well. Then I went down to the Cathedral for mass at 1pm which is the custom, and I started to see all the people who had been important to me on the trip. They were all there. The Belgians were there, the French lady was there and some Americans I had met along the way were there. So all the people that I would have wanted to meet were there at mass. It was so emotional. At the mass they ring the bells and then there are these huge incense containers that swing from one side of the Cathedral to the other; they're enormous. Then they listed all the people who had arrived that day: there were twenty from France, five from Brazil, etc. And then they mentioned the UK and there was just one, and that was me. My journey was over.'

Returning to England was tough for Linda. Being back with the truth that she was going to lose her business, her income and her home was heartwrenching. 'I realized that finishing the Camino was just the start of the real journey. It brought me back to life again. It made me appreciate the most beautiful, simple things in life. And it brought me face to face with myself and made me tackle the personal things I knew I needed to tackle. I thought going on the Camino would help me find the answers and I'd be more enlightened about the future. But it wasn't that. It basically helped me clear away the crap, and gave me a place to start the work that I needed to do.'

The Bombshell Gulp!

Collette's Story

'I think when I look back to before I became ill and before Tom died, I was going around in a daze,' recalls Collette. 'I really wasn't aware of myself or what was going on in my life. I was just so busy working, and doing all those trivial things that distract you and keep you from thinking things through on a much deeper level.'

The crisis started to unfold when Collette was thirty-one and Tom was thirty-five, and they lived in Ireland. Collette noticed a melanoma on her leg. She had it checked by a doctor and was told it was fine. So she left it. But eventually she did get quite concerned about it and went to a dermatologist. By that stage, it was already quite advanced. She had an operation to remove it and hoped it wouldn't return. But then a year later it did. It had moved to her groin area. So she had another operation. The doctors said that would be it and not to worry about it. So she went back to work, only to discover that the company was moving their whole operation over to Scotland. 'It was a really stressful time,' remembers Collette. 'We had to stay to see the transition through, but we didn't know what we were going to do next. There was so much uncertainty and stress.' It was no wonder then that six months after she was made redundant, she became very ill again. The cancer had moved to her abdominal area and caused a blockage in her bowel. She was very seriously ill this time, and the doctors gave her only four months to live.

'I didn't really believe I was going to die. It didn't even register,' says Collette. 'I was very much focused on what was going to happen next. I just thought that this was something I needed to get through.' At the same time, Tom had been quite ill himself. He'd been under a lot of pressure at work and was really stressed out and suffering from depression. 'My whole concern was about him. And my attitude to what was going on with me was that I needed to get through this to make sure he was okay. So having that external focus was extremely beneficial for me in helping me to deal with my own cancer,' recalls Collette.

Then one Monday morning, disaster struck. It was a horrible wet November day, rainy, grey and depressing. Tom was running a bit late for work and overtook a line of traffic at a place where he shouldn't have. He took a chance. And it cost him his life. He collided with a truck coming in the opposite direction and by all accounts he was killed outright.

'I was at home at the time, and I was pottering around doing my own thing,' remembers Collette. 'I kind of got this feeling and rang him at work. It wasn't that unusual really because we would speak during the day. I rang his office number and got someone strange on the phone who told me Tom wasn't at work. So feeling a little surprised I rang the switchboard and got through to his manager. His manager asked me if I was at home alone. And I replied yes, feeling a little confused. Then he told me that Tom had been in an accident and asked if I could get to the hospital.' He said not to go straight to the hospital but to pass by the office first and he would come with her. So Collette rang her parents and told them what had happened. Then she went to Tom's office to meet with his manager, as she'd promised. They sat her down and brought in two policemen. 'Even at that stage, it didn't occur to me what was going on,' says Collette. 'They told me that Tom had been in a car accident and that he hadn't made it. My response was, "What do you mean he didn't make it?" And so they really had to spell it out to me.

'It was strange. In the weeks that followed, people thought I walked around like a zombie. Yet at the same time, everything in my head was so clear and vivid. I was very much present and in the moment.'

The grieving process took time. People around her were so very supportive. Everyone looked after her, feeding her, calling her. After a while, she began to have a feeling that she needed some space alone, to be with herself and to be with Tom. 'I went to stay by the sea for a month. I needed to be by the sea and in the fresh air,' says Collette. 'And every day, I'd find myself marching up and down the beach two or three times, crying and talking to myself. It gave me permission to rant, rave and talk to myself and talk to Tom and just cry if I needed to.'

It was while she was in this space that she started to think about what was going to happen next. Tom had died, she'd lost her job and she'd just finished her last treatment for cancer, but still hadn't been given the all clear. 'When something like that happens you think, Jesus, what am I going to do now?'

Collette finally decided to study philosophy and get a Masters degree. 'I wasn't all clear on the cancer, I didn't know how long I was going to be here, so I thought, what the hell, I might as well go and do something I've always wanted to do,' she laughs. That really gave her a focus and a goal and a new set of friends. And she met people with all sorts of challenges in their life. It was good to get away from all her own stuff and be with people to talk about other things. 'Then I still didn't know what to do. But I was alive. That was a gift in itself.'

Collette was never a particularly religious person, but when Tom died she experienced and felt things that she couldn't really explain. On occasions she'd be thinking about what to do next, and this voice would come into her head as clear as day giving her instructions. It was bizarre and amazing at the same time. It was very spiritual. 'People I met, and experiences I had, just seemed to be the right people saying the right things and doing the right things at the right times. People came into my life who really helped me at just the right time.'

Looking back, Collette says, 'When you go through something like this, nothing will ever faze you and you'll cope with whatever comes along. It really does build confidence in your own ability to face a crisis with resilience.' It also made her realize that most of the stuff we do and get uptight about on a daily basis is not important at all, it's trivial. It really doesn't matter. She had to develop the ability to cut through the bullshit and just really make the decision that she didn't want this and she wasn't doing that. Rather, she wanted this and she'd have that. She had to be really clear and focused about what she wanted and what she didn't want in her life, and about who she was prepared to put up with and who she wasn't.

Collette's advice to you as you go for your Gulp! is:

- Allow yourself to be supported but don't get to be dependent on it.
- Give yourself all the time you need to deal with it.

- Feel your way through it rather than think your way through. Your positive thinking will only take you so far. Your intuition will really provide the signposts and guides for what to do.
- Pay attention to your intuition and trust your instinct.

And thankfully, Collette is still with us today.

The Breakthrough Gulp!

Dean's Story

'Joining this new company really threw me right out of my comfort zone,' says Dean, a South African living in London. 'And it really knocked my confidence. I started to doubt myself and felt lost and disoriented.' Dean had moved from a large corporation to an entrepreneurial marketing agency, and found it a real shock. Being a quiet and private person he was thrown into a client servicing role where he had to interact with people he didn't know on a daily basis. 'Normally I'd research things in depth in advance and know the nuts and bolts, and only then would I move forward,' recalls Dean. 'Instead, in this new company you were expected just to "wing it" on subjects you didn't know much about, without doing a lot of background research, and I found it really disconcerting.' Every day was a challenge for Dean as he tried to overcome his shyness and build relationships with people he didn't know very well. He felt incredibly self-conscious and awkward, especially when meeting new people when he felt under pressure to make small talk. He felt watched, and the more nervous he became, the more awkward he was and the harder he found it to have simple social conversations. He'd just freeze up. And it really undermined his confidence. 'While I was confident in some areas of my life, I was really lacking in confidence in this one,' remembers Dean. 'My normal approach obviously wasn't working, and I'd never experienced this before so it was a real shock to me. I didn't know what to do about it. But I knew that I *had* to do something about it. The question was, what?'

A long weekend break in Iceland was to be his turning point. 'I don't know what it was about Iceland,' says Dean, 'But it was like a release for me. It is just the most stunning of places, and being out in the fresh air taking photos was amazing.' And that's when Dean had one of those idle thoughts about cycling around Iceland.

But as it turned out, his next trip was not to be to Iceland, but rather to another island thousands of miles away on the other side of the world.

'It happened by pure coincidence,' recalled Dean. 'A few days after getting back from Iceland, I was cycling past Barnes railway station, and my eye caught the headline of a poster stuck to a fence saying "Cycle Around Madagascar". It was a split moment. And I stopped to read more. It was a poster about a charity ride around Madagascar to raise funds for Research Into Eating Disorders (RIED).[2] It instantly appealed to me – both the cycling and raising the £3,000 for charity.'

So, on a whim, he signed up. And for Dean, it was to prove a real challenge. But he was determined to get over his shyness, and this was one way of forcing himself to do it. Not only did he have to ask people for donations, but he'd have to spend a gruelling ten days cycling 600km in a group of forty perfect strangers. The fundraising bit alone was enough to make him break out into a sweat. He had visions of walking around the tube station with a bucket begging people for donations. 'It was my ultimate nightmare,' says Dean. 'To approach a complete stranger and ask for something. Ugh!'

But Dean soldiered on and as it turned out he managed to raise the £3,000 from donations from friends and colleagues without the need for standing in the tube station. A real achievement. But this was somewhat overshadowed by last minute nerves. 'It suddenly dawned on me what I was doing. Not only was it going to be a physical challenge, but it was going to be an emotional and mental one as well. I was really nervous about going on my own. I didn't know anybody. They were all complete strangers. It was my worst nightmare.'

And so a nervous Dean joined a bunch of strangers at Heathrow airport for the trip of a lifetime.

When I caught up with him three weeks later, he was a visibly changed man. More confident, more self-assured, and with a renewed sense of self-belief in who he was and what he stood for.

Now I don't know about you, but this is the kind of thing I might think of doing, but wouldn't really have the courage to bite the bullet and do it. I mean, a 600km cycle ride . . . that's taking it a bit too far. But there's no harm in living vicariously through Dean's adventure, so I asked him to tell me more.

Madagascar is in Southern Africa, and is the world's fourth largest island, located 250 miles off the south-east coast of Africa in the Indian Ocean east of Mozambique, and measuring slightly less than twice the size of Arizona with a population of eighteen million. It used to be a French colony, but regained independence in 1960. Dean's trip started in the capital, Antananarivo. From there they cycled through the highlands and into the rainforests. Apparently each morning the drill was the same. They woke up at around 6am (ugh!) and then had breakfast. They were on the bikes by 7am and were pedalling their way through the first twenty-five kilometres of the day before stopping for a morning break of bananas and drinks. Then another twenty-five kilometres before lunch followed by another twenty-five after lunch, before embarking on the final twenty-five kilometres to their final destination. They did that nearly every day for eight days.

'It was superb!' Dean reassures me. 'I got stronger every day. My muscles did get sore but once I got on the bike and after five minutes warming up I had this incredible sense of power and strength. The scenery was stunning as well. The first few days were hilly and then we dropped down towards the coast and had some spectacular descents. It was such a contrast, all tropical, green. Once we arrived at the coast we cycled a further 300km up the coast along some long, flat, undulating terrain. Apart from the scenery, what I remember most clearly is the people we met on the way. Madagascar is a really poor country, and you see it as you cycle through village after village of reed huts. But everyone was so friendly and the kids would run out and cheer us on as we cycled past. It was a real eye opener to see the poverty there. They have so little, yet at the same time you can see that they have this incredible satisfaction with life and are really happy and friendly. It really does make you think about what's truly important in life.'

Exhilarated and energized, the group of forty new friends arrived at the end of their journey and took the ferry to a small island called Ile Sainte Marie, best known for its beautiful beaches today, but a favourite haunt of pirates in days gone by. They spent an invigorating day cycling around the island on off-road dirt tracks, and topped it off with a rather civilized champagne lunch with barbecued king prawns (at this point Dean demonstrates the size of these prawns, and they were BIG).

Their last day together was mixed with sadness and exhilaration. It was actually Dean's birthday, and they hired quad bikes and drove like madmen around the island, visited Captain Kidd's grave at the pirate cemetery, went diving and sea kayaking and ended the evening with a beach barbecue and a boogie at the local discothèque until 3am. 'We had an absolute ball,' says Dean. 'And it was the most special birthday I've ever had. We sat on the pier and watched the sunrise. It was such a phenomenal experience.'

And all that from a chance sighting of a small poster on a fence at Barnes station.

But the question is, did Dean overcome his shyness? Did he now feel more comfortable making small talk with total strangers?

'Madagascar was not the final destination. Rather it was the first step,' says Dean emphatically. 'I was really proud of my overall achievement. I cycled 600km and I was really impressed with my fitness. I was a lot fitter and stronger than I thought I was. The big thing, though, was that I got on so well with the people there. I just remembered my core value about being genuine. And I took the attitude that I'm going to be myself and be genuine and either people will like me or they won't, and I'm not going to have any expectations around it. I just went with a genuine interest in learning about other people. And I've learnt the trick. It's much easier talking to someone about themselves than it is to talk about yourself. The nice thing about it is that I discovered I really enjoy talking to people about themselves. I learnt so many fascinating things. I got a lot out of it and it's becoming easier and easier. Now in work situations I feel more comfortable, and the conversation flows naturally. It's not as scary or traumatic as it used to be. Madagascar was a real turning point for me. I got on really well with most people. And the ones that I didn't get on with so well, it just didn't bother me. I didn't have to worry about being liked or being popular and being concerned about what people think of me. And the real bonus is that I've met some very special people and now have a whole new circle of friends.'

Looking back, I asked Dean what he learned about facing this Gulp! and stepping up to it. He laughed. 'It's shown me that you don't have to always focus on the problem at hand. There are a number of ways of getting around it. For me, the key question was, "How could I force myself outside my comfort zone, especially in the workplace?" But if I'd focused purely on that I wouldn't have been able to do what I can do now. Instead, by focusing on the cycling challenge, I was able to use that to build up my confidence, and now I am taking that new confidence back into the workplace. So I guess for me it was a case of looking at the problem from a broader perspective and looking for solutions on a much wider level. I also learnt that things don't always work out the way I'd hoped or as quickly as I wanted! I've learnt it's best to be patient and believe in myself. I've also learnt to focus on the end goal and remain flexible; concentrating on what factors I *can* influence in my life and changing them.'

Having survived his Gulp!, Dean's advice for you is simple:

- Concentrate on the positive. As long as you're heading in the right direction and breaking free of your shackles, you'll get there slowly but surely.
- Focus on living and breathing your core values. Use them as a beacon of light whenever things get tough to guide you on what actions to take.
- Surround yourself with special people with a positive outlook. You'll become more positive yourself and things will just be easier.
- Don't take things too seriously. Concentrate on doing things you enjoy.
- Set goals and take them one step at a time. Baby steps are okay.

And last, but not least, the final gem from Dean is for the shy and retiring of you:

- Talk to people about themselves. Show a genuine interest in them and they will like you for who you are, and you will discover fascinating sides to different people.

I wonder what's next for Dean?

And I wonder what's next for you?

Gulp! Action Plan: Gulp! & Go

Today's actions are simple:

Gulp! Espresso

The time has come. There's no turning back. You know it's true. Now just Gulp! and go for it.

Gulp! Mediano

No more procrastinating. No more analysing and planning. You ARE ready. Just Gulp! and go for it.

Gulp! Grande

Don't keep the next phase of your life waiting any longer. New doors will open. New opportunities will appear. It's time to move on. So just Gulp! and go for it.

Gulp! Wisdom Word

Quieten your mind and think of a number between 1 and 250.

Turn to pages 307–10 and find the word that relates to this number.

What new thoughts does this word spark?

Wisdom Word:

Epilogue

Gulp! is more than just a book. It is a philosophy. You are the creator of your life. If you come up against an obstacle, don't shy away. Face it. It's a clue. It will tell you where you need to step up and shine. This is your life, so embrace it and live it to the fullest.

My hope is that you make a Gulp! every day. It doesn't matter how big or small it is. Just do it. This will create an incredible momentum in your life, attracting new and exciting opportunities to you. You'll feel more empowered and in charge of your life. What's more, you'll open yourself for surprises to happen completely out of the blue.

And just think, if each of us made a Gulp! every day, imagine the force for change and positive momentum this would create in our world.

Gulp! Wisdom

In the place of stillness, rises potential.
From the place of potential, emerges possibility.
Where there is possibility there is choice.
And where there is choice there is freedom.

Gulp! Time

Kia Kaha. Kia Toa.
Be Strong. Be Brave.

Gulp! Wisdom Word

Quieten your mind and think of a number between 1 and 250.

Turn to pages 307–10 and find the word that relates to this number.

What new thoughts does this word spark?

Wisdom Word:

More About Gulp!

Change starts with each one of us. If you'd like to find out more about the Gulp! philosophy and be a pioneer of change across the globe then visit us on:

www.gulptime.com

Here you'll find additional resources including free downloads, inspiring stories, audio and video clips, new tips and techniques and our global community and bulletin board.

You'll also be able to keep up with the latest Gulp! news in Gabriella's personal blog as she travels the world spreading the message.

And there are zones for other Gulp! stuff, including

events near you, workshops, personal coaching, specialist courses and the charities we support.

Gulp! Stories

If you have worked through the book, stepped up to your Gulp! and transformed your life, then we want to hear about your story. It will be truly inspiring for others. Simply visit www.gulptime.com or send an email to gulpstories@gulptime.com.

Gulp! At Work

Gabriella Goddard and her team are also very passionate about bringing the Gulp! philosophy into the workplace. They can deliver Gulp! Workouts to help individuals and teams to step up to challenges within their organizations. These are particularly useful for people involved in leadership, creativity, marketing, new managers and new project kick-offs.

For more details about the Gulp! At Work programme visit www.gulptime.com or email atwork@gulptime.com

More About the Author

Gabriella Goddard is an international speaker, workshop leader, executive coach and author, and is the Managing Director of Goddard International Ltd. She is passionate about bringing spirituality out of the woo-woo arena and into the mainstream market. Her approach blends together the mind, body and soul in a way that is both insightful and practical. She created Gulp! to support people who are facing an important challenge in their lives and to help them find the courage they need to step up and face it. Gulp! is a catalyst for personal and spiritual growth.

Gabriella's background is in international marketing where she spent over fifteen years working in branding, marketing communications and new product development for both multinationals and entrepreneurial businesses in several countries. She then retrained in leadership coaching and is a graduate of the highly acclaimed Coaches Training Institute, and has studied with The Bigger Game Leadership Company in San Francisco. Originally from New Zealand, Gabriella has lived and worked in France, Japan, Mexico, Brazil and the US before settling in London, UK.

Gabriella is a popular speaker in the UK and internationally and is regularly featured in the media. She is available to speak about Gulp! at events and conferences. She is also available for selected Executive Coaching assignments for people who are serious about making a difference and being pioneers for evolving our world.

www.gulptime.com
www.gabriellagoddard.com
or
email: speaking@gulptime.com

Visit:
www.gulptime.com
for our contact address and
telephone number for your area

Notes

Acknowledgements

1. McCutchen, Julia. *The Writer's Journey: From Inspiration to Publication*, 2005. The fount of all knowledge on how to prepare your non-fiction writing for professional presentation to agents and publishers. www.ffmedia.co.uk

Introduction

1. *Kung Fu* was a popular American television series launched in 1972 by Warner Brothers.
2. *Crouching Tiger, Hidden Dragon* was a movie directed by Ang Lee in 2000, based on the book by Du Lu Wang.
3. Special thanks to Hinerau Jones who advised me on the translation from Maori to English. Hinerau and her business partner, Miriama Setterington, have created an

innovative bingo game for learning Maori vocabulary. www.classysisters.co.nz.

Additional Recommended Reading:

- Redfield, James. *The Celestine Prophecy: An Adventure*, Bantam, 1994. This was one of the first, and most influential, books I read on my spiritual journey. Watch out for the movie that goes with the book which will be out from mid-2006.

Day 1: Dare & Defy

1. Willbourne, Sian. To find out more about Sian and her 'save a life' campaign, visit www.hertssportsvillage.co.uk/savealife.html.
2. Geshe Kelsang Gyatso. *Universal Compassion: Inspiring Solutions for Difficult Times*, Tharpa Publications, 2002.
3. Pirsig, Robert M. *Zen and the Art of Motorcycle Maintenance*, Vintage, 1999.
4. Hay, Louise. *You Can Heal Your Life*, Hay House, 2002.
5. Dyer, Wayne. *Everyday Wisdom*, Hay House, 2005. A collection of over 200 of Dr Dyer's most famous quotes and observations.
6. Maslow, Abraham. *Motivation and Personality*, Longman, 1987.
7. Frankl, Viktor. *Man's Search for Meaning*, Rider & Co, 2004. The classic tribute to hope from the Holocaust.

Day 2: Breakdown & Breakthrough

1. Rowe, Dorothy. *Beyond Fear*, Harper Collins Publishers, 2002.

2. Le Doux, Joseph. *The Emotional Brain*, pages 165, 168, 194, 202, Phoenix (a division of Orion Books), 2004.
3. Goleman, Daniel. *Emotional Intelligence: Why it can matter more than IQ*, Bloomsbury, 1996.

Additional Recommended Reading:

- Jeffers, Susan. *Feel The Fear and Do It Anyway: How to Turn Your Fear and Indecision into Confidence and Action*, Arrow Books, 1991.

Day 3: Centre & Connect

1. Dickau, Jonathan, Article: *Remembering Wu-Ji*. http://jond4u.jonathandickau.com
2. Brainwave states. To learn more about the beta, alpha, theta and delta brainwave states, visit www.brainsync.com
3. Janki, Dadi. *Companion of God: The wisdom and words of one of the world's greatest spiritual leaders*, page 47, Hodder and Stoughton, 2003. www.bkwsu.com.
4. Hodgkinson, Liz. *The Story of the Brahma Kumaris: A spiritual revolution*, pages 62–7, Rider (an imprint of Ebury Press), 1999. For more information on the Brahma Kumaris, visit www.bkwsu.com
5. Tolle, Eckhart. *The Power of Now and Practising the Power of Now*, page 12, Hodder & Stoughton, 2002.
6. Lewis, Dennis. *The Tao of Natural Breathing: For health, well being and inner growth*, pages 29–42, Full Circle Publications, 2001. www.authentic-breathing.com
7. Lewis, Dennis. *Free Your Breath, Free Your Life: How conscious breathing can relieve stress, increase vitality and*

help you live more fully, pages 13–15, Shambhala Publications Inc, 2004. www.authentic-breathing.com
8. Campbell, Don. *The Mozart Effect: Tapping the power of music to heal the body, strengthen the mind and unlock the creative spirit*, pages 64-85, Hodder and Stoughton, 2002. For more information on the Mozart Effect, visit www.mozarteffect.com
9. Pearce, Stewart. *The Alchemy of Voice: Transform and enrich your life through the power of your voice*, Hodder and Stoughton, 2005. For more information about your signature note, visit Stewart's website at www.thealchemyofvoice.com
10. Cohen, Michael. *Reconnecting With Nature: Finding Wellness Through Restoring Your Bond With The Earth*, Ecopress, 1997. www.ecopsych.com
11. Chief Seattle. For more information on Chief Seattle and the Pacific northwest coast culture and art, visit www.chiefseattle.com

Additional Recommended Reading:

- Robson, Rich. Article: *Wu Chi – The Power of Stillness.* www.kungfusandiego.com
- Chu, Vincent. Article: *A Discussion on Wu Chi.*
- Master Lam Kam Chuen. *The Way of Energy. Mastering the Chinese Art of Internal Strength with Chi Kung Exercise*, Gaia Books Ltd, 1991. See page 28 for explanation of Wu-Chi.
- Master Lam Kam Chuen. *The Way of Power. Reaching Full Strength in Body and Mind*, Gaia Books Ltd, 2003. See page 26 for explanation of Wu-Chi.

Day 4: Imagine & Invent

1. Green, Soleira. *The Alchemical Coach Handbook: The Alchemy of Passion, Power and Potential*, published by S.O.U.L. Ltd, 2005. Also, visit The Evolutionary Institute to learn about cutting edge training on developing your visionary potential. www.evolutionaryinstitute.com
2. Wright brothers. To find out more about the pioneers of the aero industry, visit www.first-to-fly.com, for history, photos and quotes.
3. MacArthur, Ellen. *Race Against Time*, Michael Joseph Ltd, 2005. *Taking On the World*, Penguin, 2003.
4. Leden, Judy. *Flying With Condors: Hanggliding and Paragliding Champion of the World*, Orion, 1996.
5. Roddick, Anita. *Business As Unusual: Profits With Principles*, Anita Roddick Publishing, 2005.
6. Oliver, Jamie. For more information on Jamie Oliver's campaign for better school dinners for our children, visit www.feedmebetter.com

Day 5: Plan & Prepare

1. Dyer, Wayne. *The Power of Intention: Change the Way you Look at Things and the Things you Look at Will Change*, page 86, Hay House, 2004.
2. *What the BLEEP! Do We Know*? For more information on the movie and the community building around it, visit www.whatthebleep.com
3. Grant, Anthony and Greene, Jane. *Solution Focused Coaching: Managing People in a Complex World*, Momentum, 2003.

4. Loehr, Jim and Schwartz, Tony. *The Power of Full Engagement: Managing Energy, Not Time, Is the Key to High Performance and Personal Renewal*, Free Press, 2005.

Day 6: Focus & Flow

1. Overton, Patrick. Author of the 'Faith' Poem. www.patrickoverton.com
2. Alexander Technique. The complete guide to the Alexander Technique can be found at www.alexandertechnique.com.
3. *The Washington Post*, 8 January, 2005, page C01. 'A Sense Of Doom: Animal Instinct For Disaster', by Don Oldenburg. Information on how animals' sixth sense helped save them from death during the 2004 Tsunami that hit South East Asia.
4. Churchill Fellowships are offered by The Winston Churchill Memorial Trust, www.wcmt.org.uk
5. Jung, Carl Gustav. *Synchronicity: An Acausal Connecting Principle*, Princeton University Press, 1974.
6. Chopra, Deepak. *Synchrodestiny: Harnessing the infinite power of coincidence to create miracles*, page 121, Rider, 2003.
7. Lorenz, Edward. *The Essence of Chaos*, Routledge, an imprint of Taylor & Francis Books Ltd, 1996. Also, Gleick, J, *CHAOS: Making a New Science*, New York: Penguin Books, 1987.
8. Geshe Kelsang Gyatso. *Transform Your Life: A Blissful Journey*, Tharpa Publications, 2001.
9. To find out more about Alchemy and the Alchemists, visit www.levity.com/alchemy/, a site organized by Adam McLean, a well-known authority on alchemical

texts and symbolism, author and publisher of over forty books on alchemical and Hermetic ideas.

10. To learn about how you can use energy healing techniques to transform emotions visit www.emotrance.com

Additional Recommended Reading

- Hodge, Stephen. *Zen Masterclass: A course in Zen wisdom from traditional masters*, Godsfield Press, 2002.
- Belitz, Charlene and Lundstrom, Meg. *The Power of Flow: Practical Ways to Transform Your Life With Meaningful Coincidence*, Three Rivers Press, 1998.

Day 7: Gulp! & Go

1. Davies, Bethan and Cole, Ben. *Walking the Camino El Santiago*, Pili Pala Press, 2003. www.pilipalapress.com/camino. Also, MacLaine, Shirley. *The Camino: A Pilgrimage of Courage*, Pocketbooks, 2001.
2. For more information on Research Into Eating Disorders (RIED) and their fundraising challenges to Madagascar, Chile and Vietnam, contact the Institute of Psychiatry, King's College London, UK.

Wisdom Words

1 'No Thing'
2 Achieve
3 Action
4 Action Plan
5 Adventure
6 Alchemize
7 Alert
8 Alignment
9 Apparent
10 Attachment
11 Attitude
12 Awareness
13 Balance
14 Barrier
15 Be Brave
16 Be Confident
17 Be Curious
18 Be Daring
19 Be Free
20 Be Heard
21 Be Present
22 Be Proud
23 Begin
24 Beliefs
25 Believe
26 Benefits
27 Best Case
28 Bigger Picture
29 Blocks
30 Boundaries
31 Break Out
32 Breakdown
33 Breakthrough
34 Breathe
35 Broaden
36 Bubbling Up
37 Build
38 Calm
39 Catalyst
40 Centre
41 Certainty
42 Chance
43 Chaos
44 Chit Chat
45 Choose
46 Clarity
47 Co-create
48 Coincidence
49 Collaborate
50 Comfort Zone

51 Commence
52 Commitment
53 Concentrate
54 Conditioning
55 Confidence
56 Connect
57 Contrast
58 Contribute
59 Control
60 Conviction
61 Core
62 Courage
63 Create
64 Create Space
65 Creator
66 Curiosity
67 Dare
68 Decide
69 Deep Down
70 Defend
71 Define
72 Defy
73 Demystify
74 Denial
75 Direction
76 Discover
77 Dissolve
78 Dream
79 Drive
80 Dynamic
81 Easy
82 Elevate
83 Eliminate
84 Embark
85 Embrace
86 Emotion
87 Empty
88 Energy
89 Enthusiasm
90 Essence
91 Evaluate
92 Evolve
93 Examine
94 Expand
95 Experience
96 Fear
97 Feeling
98 First Steps
99 Flow
100 Focus
101 Follow
102 Footbridges
103 Foundations
104 Fun
105 Fundamental
106 Future
107 Gain
108 Gaps
109 Get Started
110 Glow
111 Go
112 Go For It!
113 Gracefully
114 Grounded
115 Grow
116 Guide
117 Guilt
118 Gulp!
119 Head
120 Heart
121 Identity
122 Illuminate
123 Illusion
124 Imagine

125 Impact
126 Impetus
127 Implement
128 Important
129 In the Flow
130 Inner Talk
131 Inspiration
132 Instinctive
133 Integrate
134 Intention
135 Interact
136 Interconnection
137 Intuition
138 Invent
139 Inventive
140 Journey
141 Kindness
142 Lead
143 Leap
144 Leap of Faith
145 Learn
146 Leave a Trail
147 Lesson
148 Let Go
149 Liberate
150 Lightness
151 Listen
152 Luck
153 Magic
154 Master
155 Meaning
156 Meaningful
157 Meditate
158 Miracle
159 Move Forward
160 Music
161 Natural
162 Nature
163 Necessity
164 Needs
165 New Eyes
166 Next Level
167 No
168 No Ego
169 Notice
170 Observe
171 On Target
172 On Track
173 Open
174 Opportunity
175 Order
176 Out of the Box
177 Paint a Picture
178 Paradigm Shift
179 Pathway
180 Perception
181 Persist
182 Perspective
183 Pioneer
184 Pivot Point
185 Poise
186 Positive
187 Possibility
188 Potential
189 Practise
190 Prepare
191 Purpose
192 Quantum Leap
193 Question
194 Rational
195 Reacting
196 Reality
197 Reconnect
198 Reflect

199 Resistance
200 Responsibility
201 Responsible
202 Reverse
203 Risk
204 Role Model
205 Safe
206 Seek
207 Sense
208 Sensible
209 Separate
210 Serendipity
211 Shine
212 Signposts
213 Silence
214 Silver Lining
215 Simplicity
216 Smart
217 Space
218 Spark
219 Sparkle
220 Specific
221 Spirit
222 Spontaneous
223 Status Quo
224 Step Out
225 Step Up
226 Stillness
227 Stop
228 Strength
229 Stretch
230 Strive
231 Strong
232 Stuck
233 Success
234 Swiftly
235 The Void
236 Think Differently
237 Timing
238 Transform
239 Triggers
240 True Nature
241 Trust
242 Truth
243 Uncertainty
244 Unknown
245 Upside Down
246 Values
247 Vibrant
248 Visualize
249 Wisdom
250 Yes